The Triple Tree

Newgate, Tyburn and Old Bailey

Donald Rumbelow

Harrap London

To

K. Arne Blom

First published in Great Britain 1982
by HARRAP LIMITED
19-23 Ludgate Hill, London EC4M 7PD

© *Donald Rumbelow* 1982

ISBN 0 245-53877-1

Designed by Robert Wheeler
Filmset by Martin's Printing Works, Berwick upon Tweed
Printed and bound in Great Britain by
R. J. Acford, Chichester

Contents

Acknowledgments

I would like to thank the following for their generous help and assistance:

Frank Atkinson; John Clark, Senior Assistant Keeper, Department of Medieval Antiquities at the Museum of London; Adrian Eatwell; Joe Gaute; Ralph Hyde, the Keeper of Prints and Maps, and his assistant, John Fisher, at the Corporation of the City of London; Miss Betty Masters, the Deputy Keeper of Records at the City of London; Pat Plank and Ray Hodges at the Commissioner's Library, New Scotland Yard; Roger Sheppard; Molly Whittington-Egan; K Arne Blom who nursed it to Swedish publication; my editor Simon Dally; Michael Shaw—as always; Cherry Hadley, Mother General and Mother John Baptist at the Tyburn Convent; Museum of London; National Portrait Gallery; lastly, to my family who have put up with the long absences and ruined weekends.

The publishers and author wish to thank the following sources for permission to reproduce the illustrations: British Museum 117; City of London Police 53; Guildhall Library 16, 28, 29, 39, 43, 45, 46, 50, 59, 61, 69, 70, 75, 80-81, 100, 105, 135, 142, 143, 146, 147, 159, 168, 172-3, 178 (t), 187, 213; Museum of London 79, 196, 198; National Portrait Gallery 91, 123, 133; Press Association 214, 215. Other illustrations were supplied by the author.

Introduction

This vulgar notion is sometimes expressed by words to the following effect:
'The power of the law consists in its terrors; if you wholly cease to hang, the common people will have nothing to fear: therefore hang one now and then'.

Edward Gibbon Wakefield, Facts relating to the punishment of death in the metropolis, 2nd edition (1832)

But be it payne or nat: there many suche ende.
At Newgate theyr garmentis are offred to be solde.
Theyr bodyes to the Jebet solemly ascende,
Wauynge with the wether whyle theyr necke wyl holde.

Alexander Barclay, The Ship of Fools, 1509

The Triple Tree referred to is the triangular shaped gallows that stood at Tyburn for over 200 years on the main west road out of London. In popular imagery it was the Deadly Never-Green, the Three-Legged Mare, the Fatal Tree. A triangular gallows meant that eight people could swing side by side from each beam at once, twenty-four at a time. Spectators were case-hardened to such sights, and could regard such deaths with equanimity; hanging to them was 'only a kick', or 'a wry neck and a wet pair of breeches'.

The book is divided into three sections: the prison, the gallows, and the court. Each section can be read as one leg of the Triple Tree: Newgate, Tyburn and the Old Bailey. When Tyburn evolved at the end of the twelfth century it did so at the same time as the great gaol of Newgate, and the story of one is the story of both. The Old Bailey, which is what is generally meant by the Central Criminal Court, was a much later development of the nineteenth century but in the context of this book can be taken as referring to the much earlier Sessions House which stood on the same site adjoining the prison. The categories are very broad ones but it has proved impossible to make a sharp division between them. Inevitably there has been overlapping. Broadly speaking, Newgate deals with the history of the prison building itself, and the keepers and turnkeys who had the ordering of it; Old Bailey is the treatment of the prisoners, their escapes and trials; the last section on Tyburn is concerned with the hangmen, the superstitions, and executions not only at Tyburn but at Newgate as well.

'Gaylors buying theire offices will deale hardly with pitifull prisoners' was another way of saying that behind the theories of reform the day-to-day administrators of Newgate were more concerned with their own interests than in reforming society or the criminal. This bleak conclusion is what emerges most clearly from the documentation of several centuries. Occasionally there are glimmers of hope that changes might be occurring for the better as a result of a different attitude of the prison-keepers or of the work of reformers such as John Howard and Elizabeth Fry.

But, almost without exception, within two or three decades one finds a regression to the old ways and abuses; although it is claimed they had been stamped-out, particularly in the Select Committee papers of the nineteenth century, they are still continued and flourished, though in an amended form. Some of their continuance can be directly attributed to the self-interest not only of the keepers, turnkeys and chaplains, but perversely to the prisoners themselves who exploited each other. Self-interest was true of the hangmen even as late as 1885, in the last days of Newgate, when the Town Clerk's office was flooded with applications for the post of hangman, including one from the Bradford-based hangman James Berry, who wrote that in the fourteen months since he had been hangman he had hanged about twenty-four persons out of forty-nine, the others being reprieved. His uncertainty about the exact number he had hanged was due to the bungled execution of John Lee who was three times put on the drop—it failed to work even though Berry stamped on the flaps to make them fall. The reason why the machinery failed to work has always been a matter of controversy. Only days after his application Berry wrote again asking for the matter to be settled, as if he did not get the regular salary he would have to move from his home at 1 Bilton Place, which he referred to as the Executioner's Office, to one where he would pay less rent! His letter has the echoes of a hangman nearly 200 years before who, because there had been so few executions, petitioned for something to keep himself from starving, he being 'ffitt for no other imployment'.

Such pragmatism seems more typical of Dark Ages penology where death, outlawry, mutilation and monetary compensation were the punishments decreed by law and the beginnings of a prison system only just stirring in the laws of Alfred.

> The amount of compensation to be paid in each case was carefully stipulated and carefully graded. While a murderer might have to pay a hundred shillings, the compensation was limited to twenty shillings if the assailant only succeeded in smashing his enemy's chin bone. Every part of the body had its value, from fifty shillings for an eye or a foot to sixpence for a toe-nail. Injuries which interfered with a man's ability to work or fight were compensated at a higher rate than those which disfigured him. The loss of a thumb, for instance, was deemed to be worth twenty shillings and a disabled shoulder thirty shillings, but the loss of an ear was worth twelve shillings and a front tooth six shillings. To break a man's thigh cost twelve shillings and to cut off his little finger, eleven; but to lacerate his ear cost only six. To injure his power of speech cost the same as to break three of his ribs. To pierce his penis cost six shillings compensation, but to break both his collar bones cost twelve.

The theft of Church property, being God's property, had to be compensated twelve times over. Some crimes such as murder and arson could not always be compensated and were punished by death or mutilation. The Church in fact favoured the substitution of mutilation for the death penalty as this gave the offender the chance to expiate his crime. Hangings were often carried out on the borders of towns and settlements—a practice apparently continued through from the Dark Ages to the eighteenth century when the southeast leg of Tyburn gallows was used to fix the boundary mark of St George's, Hanover Square.

By the tenth century a more vicious penal code was coming into being. Crime was not being checked by mutilation and death; and the reason for this failure, so it seemed, was that the punishments were not savage enough. A greater severity was required; after the Conquest this can best be typified by the savage Forest Laws of

William I, where death was not to be instantaneous but had to be preceded by mutilation. At the same time there is an extension of the private prisons in castles and fortified places, and also the evolving of the modern prison system by the sheriffs, who had the responsibility of bringing prisoners to trial. From the stocks and makeshift cells which they resorted to evolved the modern prison. Increased harshness of the law, and the building of strong places where pre-trial prisoners could be held, evolved at much the same time and together spawned what is probably the greatest gaol of them all—a place which no prisoner ever thought of as anything but a 'soore streite and perillous prisone for any man to be yn'.

The
Prison

After we had shot the Arch, we turned up a Street, which my Companion told me was the Old-Bailey. We walk'd on till we came to a great Pair of Gates; it being a remarkable Place, according to my usual Custom, I requested my Friend to give me some further Knowledge of the matter, who informed me it was Justice-Hall, where a Dooms-day Court was held once a Month to Sentence such Canary-Birds to a Penitential Psalm, who will, rather be choak'd by the Product of Hemp-seed, for living Roguishly, than exert their Power in Lawful Labour, to purchase their Bread Honestly. In this narrow part of the Street (says my friend) into which we are now passing, many a such Wretch has taken his last Walk; for we are going towards that famous University, where, if a Man has a mind to Educate a hopeful Child in the Daring Science of Padding; the Light-Finger's Subtlety of Shop-Lifting; the excellent use of Jack and Crow, for the silently drawing Bolts, and forcing Barricadoes; with the Knack of Sweetning; or the most Ingenious Dexterity of Picking Pockets; let him but enter him in this College on the Common Side, and Confine him close to his Study but for three Months; and if he does not come out Qualified to take any Degree of Villainy; he must be the most Honest Dunce that ever had the Advantage of such Eminent Tutors.

The London Spy Revived, 1699

Whoever is obliged, or chooses to attend the trials of criminals, especially in crowded courts, should begin by first resolving most courageously, not to be affected with the least dread of whatever he may smell or feel; by the direction of his physicians, he should prudently empty his stomach and bowels a few days before, to carry off any putrid or putrescent substance which may have lodged in them; and this is done very easily by a suitable mild purge. The diet which such persons should observe, is the mere abstaining from all gross, heavy, spicy, and viscid food; by eating well-dressed, light meats, and drinking in moderation, of true cordial wines, as claret, port, and old hock; brandy or rum punch acidulated with oranges, lemons, limes, or tamarinds, so as to exhilerate, promote a general perspiration, and prevent dejection of the mind, or lassitude of the body. By such means it is likely no one need fear infection, or shrink from his duty. . .

Directions to prevent the contagion of the
jail-distemper commonly called the jail-fever.
London, 1772.

Roman fort

To the legions trying to hold down the outposts of the Roman Empire the island of Britannia was 'ferox provincia' (a warlike province) resisting the invader, in the words of one chronicler, with 'slaughter, the gibbet, fire and the cross'. Among the casualties of the Boudiccan revolt was the small trading settlement on the north bank of the Thames where the invading legions had thrown a bridge across the river some twenty years before. Inhabitants who were unable to struggle westwards after the retreating legions were abandoned to their fate, like the settlement, which was reduced to ashes; women's breasts were sewn to their lips; heads were struck off with iron swords and others used in nameless tribal rites. Rome tightened its grip on the province once more. The uprising was crushed. The settlement was rebuilt and a fort, covering some twelve acres of land, enough for a garrison of 2,000 men, was built to protect it; it was this hill-fort (Londinium) which gave the settlement its name. Later, a wall, some two miles long, was built around the settlement as added protection; it curved round from the foreshore, like the arch of a bow, with the river as its draw-string.

In the centuries that followed, in the ebb and flow of conquest, this wall, like a belt, was to restrict the City's growth, though the buildings within it were to change constantly, a temple to bull-slaying Mithras giving way to a cathedral to St Paul.

As part of the defences a V-shaped moat was dug around the wall; it varied in depth from fourteen to twenty-two feet deep. On the west the ground outside the wall sloped away to a fleet or creek (later to be named the Fleet River) which flowed parallel to the wall as it turned south to the river; this section of wall had two gates, Newgate and Ludgate, (these are their later names as their Roman names are unknown). Possibly Newgate was already known by its ninth-century name of 'Westgetum'—the gate to the west. On the far side of the Fleet, and in other places outside the wall, were cemeteries where the Romans buried their dead; interments were forbidden inside the walls and punished by a fine of forty aurei.

There were seven main gates into the City. The wall's imposing facade was a mixture of rough-hewn Kentish ragstone and bonding tiles held together by a grey and sometimes reddish-coloured cement which misled a later chronicler into thinking that the stones had been 'tempered with the blood of beasts'. The gatehouse at Newgate was a two-storey building with a bridge opening out onto the ditch. The upper storey may have had a flat roof and battlements where look-outs could be posted. The bottom storey was divided into two, with guardrooms on either side, about thirty-five feet apart, separated by twin tunnels through which travellers, coming or going, had to pass.

Even after the legions had been recalled to Rome and the City had subsided into a 'slum of decaying buildings in which past greatness could be more readily discerned than any future promise', this basic gate structure seems to have remained unchanged. Becket's clerk, William Fitzstephen, in his twelfth-century *Descriptio Londonia*, says of the strength of the City:

> On the east stands the Palatine tower, a fortress of great size and strength, the court and walls of which are erected upon a very deep foundation, the mortar used in the building being tempered with the blood of beasts. On the west are two castles strongly fortified; the wall of the city is high and thick, with *seven double gates,* having on the north side towers placed at proper intervals.

South of Newgate, no distance away, was Ludgate; in Fitzstephen's time the ground behind it sloped up to the great west doors of St Paul's. The stretch of wall between the two gates was the bailey, a medieval expression for the walls or defences which surround the keep. Possibly it was the outwork, part of the great bank of earth that had been built up against the

Roman Newgate: a reconstruction by Alan Sorrell.

inside wall, that was referred to in 1423 as 'the mud wall in the grete bayli' in need of repair. From the twelfth century onwards there are references to terra de Bali (*c.* 1166), le Bail, le Baille (1311), la Ballie (1287), Le Bayl (1290), La Baillye (1431), the grete bayli (1423), and the earliest reference to Old Baily (1444). The name recurs again as the Olde bailly (1481), tholde Baylye (1549), Old Balee (Bayle) (1556). The prefix was probably added to differentiate it from a side street called Little Bayly which didn't finally disappear until *c.* 1760 when a block of houses was pulled down and the combined streets were called by the one name of Old Bailey.

Gaol of London

Prisons, in the modern context, are first referred to in the laws of Alfred in the ninth century. Pillorying, death, mutilation and outlawry were commonplace punishments and prisons were no more than places of detention where prisoners could be detained for trial or sentence. Possibly, in this pre-trial period, a 'prison' was little more than a pair of stocks boxed in with timber and similar to the 'small howsis' that were built at the beginning of the sixteenth century by the City's wards to offer some shelter to 'sterk beggars and vagabundys' that had been laid by the heels. Churchman and noble had their own prisons. The 'Bishop's' prison in St Paul's continued in existence long after other lay prisons had disappeared by the end of the fourteenth century.

It was on church ground, on the banks of the Fleet which flowed parallel to the west wall, that London's first prison was built. The exact date of its building is uncertain but probably it was about the year 1130. Its importance was emphasized by references to it as 'the gaol of London'. Astonishingly it did not maintain its pre-eminence for long. The reason for its supplantation is hard to explain, unless it is seen as a pawn in the growing conflict between the claims of Church and State which was to culminate within this same period with the death of Becket. The ground, on which the Fleet prison stood, was part of the possessions of the ancient See of Canterbury. The adaptation of Newgate to a prison may have been one of the consequences of this conflict. Certainly the gates, and the rooms above them, were not the dilapidated structures that one might imagine; their occupancy was much sought after and as late as the fourteenth century they were frequently tenanted by members of the mayor's household. One mayoral official petitioned that his wife might be allowed to continue her tenure in the rooms over Aldersgate, where he had made substantial improvements even to the extent of setting up 'dyvers newe houses as parlours Chambres with bay wyndows and other houses of office' at his own cost. Whatever the reason for its conversion, Newgate in its early years was a royal prison and remained so, despite protests from the Londoners, jealous as ever of their rights and privileges, that they alone could have a lawful prison within the walls. It was not until Henry IV's usurpation of the throne that the prison, and the cost of maintaining it, was conceded to them in a conciliatory gesture.

The date of Newgate's change from a guard-house to a prison is not known but occurred between the building of the Fleet (*c*.1130) and the purchase of a piece of land by the side of the gate in 1187-8 for specific use as a gaol site; two carpenters and a smith were paid £36 0*s* 11*d* for work carried out. More work and repairs continued to be carried out for the next thirty years. Arguably, the slowness of the work was due to slowness of payment; and the reluctance of the two City sheriffs who had the overall responsibility of the prison to carry out repairs suggests that they had some difficulty in being reimbursed for their expenses. In 1218, in the reign of Henry III, they were promised that the costs would be borne by the Royal Exchequer. Eighteen years later, on a specific command from the King that certain prisoners should be confined in one of the turrets, nearly £100 was expended in converting the turret into cells.

Persons who were thought dangerous to the Crown or to the state were brought to Newgate from as far afield as Oxfordshire, Lincolnshire and Warwickshire. Some counties were without prisons and had no place to keep prisoners; in 1259 Newgate was put at the disposal of the Sheriff of Essex because he had no prison of his own. State prisoners, foreign hostages and traitors were brought to Newgate for safe keeping.

Since Newgate was a royal prison it followed that there had to be a more general prison for the Londoners themselves. The adjoining gateway of Ludgate was adapted to this purpose though there was never the same scale of rebuilding. Primarily it was a prison for freemen who were being held for debt, trespass or contempt. Persons charged with more serious crimes were stripped of their freedom and committed to Newgate. Conditions were not harsh and in 1419 Ludgate was ordered to be closed because so many debtors preferred to be arrested and confined there rather than pay their debts. Living conditions were equally palatable in the two debtors' compters of Bread Street and Poultry, so much so that in 1431 an order had to be made that prisoners should not be kept in either place for more than one day and night before being committed to Newgate.

Ludgate's closure was only temporary. Conditions were so appalling that within four months it had to be reopened because so many had died who, as was admitted, might have been living still had it not been for the 'fetid and corrupt atmosphere that is in the heynhouse gaol of Newgate'.

Governing of the gaol

Considering the close proximity of the prisons to each other, it is not immediately easy to grasp why deaths should have been so much higher in one prison than the other unless the shifts in shrieval and prison official responsibility are grasped. Much of the inhumanity that persisted within Newgate over several centuries is directly attributable to its administration, which remained much the same well into the nineteenth century.

The Sheriffs

The administrative responsibility for Newgate and the City's other prisons belonged to the two sheriffs who were part of the aldemanic governing body and elective heirs to the mayoral office, the post of sheriff being one step below. Each of these high offices would be held for twelve months. On the day they assumed office the old and new sheriffs were instructed to 'go together to the prison of Newgate, and there the new sheriffs shall receive all the prisoners by indenture made between them and the old Sheriffs, and shall place due safeguard there at their own peril, without letting the gaol to ferm'. In a formal handing over, the mayor gave 'the cocket' or seal of Newgate and its keys to one of the sheriffs who retained custody of both until the Vigil of St Michael (28th February) when they were returned. From 1327 the mayor was an ex-officio justice of the gaol delivery of Newgate although he had no responsibility for the safe-keeping of the prisoners which remained with the sheriffs.

Clearly, as can be seen from the above, the sheriffs were not conventional prison officers but political representatives who, by overseeing the prisons, were carrying out but one part of their official duties. Since the eleventh century, and possibly before, they had had an official responsibility for bringing suspects to trial. Both before and after the construction of purpose-built gaols, they were sometimes forced to adapt a part of their private house to a prison and in other cases—since they were justiciars as well—to add a court-room for cases to be tried. Parts of the City's Guildhall had to be adapted in a similar manner. In the counties, as late as the eighteenth century, 'Anything might serve, from the cellar of an inn to the gatehouse of an abbey'.

Day-to-day administration devolved upon the keeper whom the sheriffs appointed. The sheriffs' instructions were not to 'let the Gaol of Newgate to ferm, but shall put there a man, sufficient and of good repute, to keep the said gaol in due manner, without taking anything of him for such Keeping thereof, by covenant made in private, or openly'. This was ignored, as for each prisoner who escaped the sheriffs could be fined one hundred shillings and if a debtor escaped they could be sued for his debt as well. To protect himself the keeper had to put up a bond on appointment which made him liable instead. Even this did not stop the sheriffs from being punished in 1255 when a prisoner escaped who had killed a prior who was cousin to the Queen. Possibly using this as an excuse to punish the City generally, which had been critical of his policies, the King imprisoned the sheriffs, fined the City 3,000 marks and outlawed the gaoler for five years.

Despite the strictures on the selling of places, it is clear that keepers did buy their way into office and that the money, or at least a part of it, was used to defray the mayor's and sheriffs' expenses when in office. In 1694 this process was accelerated when the City went bankrupt and was officially declared so by Act of Parliament. In order to recoup its losses the City sold a whole range of offices by auction, including attorneys in the sheriff's court, bailiffs, barge-masters, masons, clerks and keepers of the prisons. In some instances these sales continued through to the early nineteenth century. According to a list of offices bought and sold in 1696 'according to the best information which can at present be got' the keeper's office was sold for £2,500; another contemporary source says that the sum involved was £3,500. By this date, other evidence not available, the keeper's office was entirely at the disposal of the Lord Mayor and sheriffs. The bulk of the purchase money obviously went to the outgoing keeper but a certain percentage went to the Lord Mayor and sheriffs. In 1708 William Pitt paid them £105, which was the agreed one-third of the purchase price of £315 that he had to pay for the post of Master Keeper on its surrender by James Fell. This clipping of percentages applied to a whole range of other offices which were at the Lord Mayor's and sheriffs' disposal. The official fugures were published in 1747 by the City which itself took one-third of the amount declared. Collectively, and it must be emphasized not individually, between 1704 and 1747 successive Lord Mayors and sheriffs pocketed between them £92,827 19s. 10d. and the City a more modest £46,413 19s. 11d.

Gradually the City bought back the offices they had been forced to sell. When the keeper's place fell vacant in 1734 they would not let the Lord Mayor and the sheriffs dispose of it by auction, but recommended that they should be paid £1,000 in compensation for their 'pretension' to dispose of the office which for the future should be disposed of by them by appointment.

It can hardly be coincidental that with this radical change the beginnings of reform start to stir.

The Keeper

The day-to-day working of Newgate itself was pivoted on the keeper. According to *Liber Albus:*

> The Gaoler, who by the said Sheriffs shall be deputed thereunto, shall make oath before the Mayor and Aldermen that neither he, nor any other for him, shall take fine, or extortionate charge, from any prisoner for putting on, or taking off his irons, or shall receive monies extorted from any prisoner. But it shall be fully lawful for the said gaoler to take from each person, when set at liberty, four pence for his fee, as from ancient times has been the usage; but he shall take from no person at his entrance there, nor shall he issue (execution) suddenly, by command of the Mayor and Aldermen without other process. And if he shall be found to commit extortion upon anyone, he shall be ousted from his office, and be punished at the discretion of the Mayor and Aldermen and Common Council of the City.

In 1440 the sheriffs were charged with the responsibility of appointing and paying the custodians of Newgate and Ludgate. As already mentioned, the keeper had to put up a bond when appointed which made him liable for the sheriff's fines and debts of prisoners who escaped. As he was also responsible for the prison's repairs, it follows that to clear himself, and to turn a profit, money had to be exacted from the only remaining source, which was the prisoners themselves. It was a hard but true saying that 'Gaylors buying theire offices will deale hardly with pitifull prisoners'. Callousness was the least of their virtues. According to an entry in the City's Journal on 15 March 1447, James Mannyng, Keeper of the Gaol of Newgate, 'on Saturday last wickedly and negligently permitted the bier of a dead prisoner to stand in the King's Highway, causing a nuisance and great danger to the King who was passing there: And because he was obstinate after many admonitions made to him, and of shameful words spoken by his wife, to have nine days in the compter.' One of his successors, only two years later, William Arnold, was committed to one of the sheriffs' compters, and to remain there at the discretion of the mayor, because he had committed a dreadful assault on one of the women prisoners in his custody.

This was to be a familiar pattern of brutality, extortion and corruption. Prisoners were helpless, unnecessarily chained and with little chance of redress. Special commissions in 1319 and again in 1333 emphasize that such abuses were of long standing and continued to be, though from time to time the keepers were punished with dismissal, fines or token imprisonment in one of the compters.

Prisoners had to pay for basic services. In 1393 the Court of Common Council, the City's governing body, ordered that prisoners should not be charged for beds and lamps nor pay him more than fourpence for their discharge; the facts show that the prisoners were being made to pay fees when they came into the prison or one shilling more than the fourpence which was the normal fee when they were discharged. This order did give prisoners some right of redress if they could prove the charges against the keeper—he could be fined ten times the sum he had exacted, half of which was to be paid to the City and half to the complainant. Another long-standing abuse was the unnecessary ironing and manacling of prisoners; in theory, this might have been done to stop them escaping but the practice shows that it was done so that the keeper could exact the equivalent 100 shillings that he was under bond to the sheriffs to pay for each prisoner that escaped. This money, like so much else, became part of his perquisites.

In the sixteenth and seventeenth centuries men and women who had been imprisoned for their religious beliefs, whether they were Catholic, Protestant, Quaker or Nonconformist, were treated equally as badly though sometimes there is the odd glimmer of humane treatment from the occasional keeper. Catholics who were held in Newgate from 1612 to 1621 for refusing to take the oath of allegiance were allowed considerable freedom, even to the extent of saying mass, by the keeper, Simon Houghton, whose wife was a Catholic convert. Eventually his toleration was discovered and he was prosecuted for gross neglect of duty. His successor, as the prisoners quickly complained, swiftly brought them back to a stricter control and a starvation diet more in keeping with the gaolers of thirty years before who levied fines, and took bribes. In one instance, a husband and wife were complained of as 'most horrible blasphemers and swearers'.

Conditions deteriorated further as the City grew steadily more bankrupt and the buying and selling of offices became more blatant. Just how gross the malpractices had become is evident from a pamphlet published in 1680 by Elizabeth Cellier called *Malice Defeated*. According to the sub-title it had been written 'for the satisfaction of all Lovers of undisguised Truth'. Even though she overstates her case and relies a great deal on hearsay, her revelations of conditions in Newgate were enough to alarm the authorities; they brought her to trial and fined her the considerable sum of £1,000, not because of what she said, but because she had dared to publish. Some, but not many, of her allegations were rebutted in court by the keeper himself, who angrily denied that he possessed a set of irons called the 'Sheers', which weighed forty pounds and which were used to iron certain prisoners. He challenged few of her other statements which, if exaggerated, certainly had some foundation in fact. She alleged:

> There have been many more cruel things acted in that Mansion of Horror, as the Story they tell of one Captain Clarke, who being Prisoner only for Debt, was locked up in a little dark hole two days and two Nights, having no other company but the Quarters of two Executed persons, the extream stench of which had perhaps kill'd him, had he not took the miserable relief of holding a foul Chamber Pot to his Nose.

Another prisoner was Elizabeth Evans whom the gaoler ordered to the Condemned Room, double ironed and kept in isolation and without sustenance: '. . . and then the Jaylor thought fit to employ some other Engines of his Tyranny, amongst which, was a certain thing (by him called a Cap of Maintenance), which was fixed to her head with a thing like the Rowel of a Spur, being put in her Mouth, cleaves to the Roof with such extream Torture, that is not to be exprest; this the Woman endured several times, till at last, by making her Address to some good people, and telling the manner of her usage, they did contribute to the Gaolers demands, and so she with great difficulty obtained her Liberty.'

Much of the blame for these continuing abuses must be fairly laid on the City authorities themselves who resignedly turned a blind eye to such malpractices by arguing: 'The officers buy their places, and therefore 'tis Reasonable in them they should make the best of them.' James Whiston, in

Fetters, irons and torture instruments taken from the Marshalsea prison in 1720. Mrs Cellier alleged that similar instruments were used in Newgate.

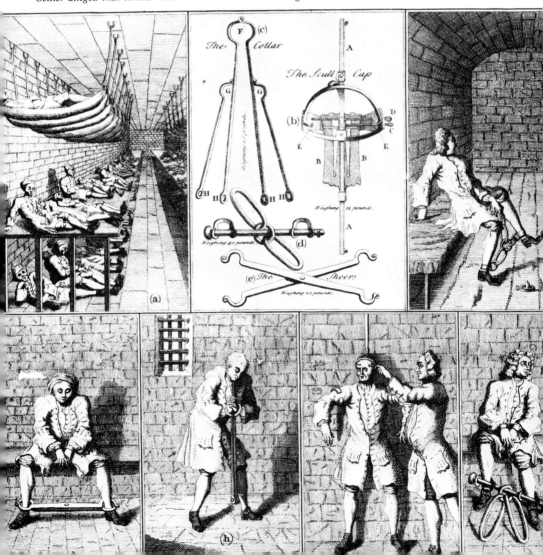

his book *England's Calamities discovered*, was fiercely critical of this attitude:

> It is by this means that purchased cruelty grows bold, and plumes itself in its extortion. . . . It is example that corrupts us all; for how commonly do the under officers, gaolers, &c., excuse their barbarity and unreasonable exactions, in alleging that they have no other way to make up the interest of their purchase money? . . . It is this alone that steels and casehardens a gaoler's conscience against all the pity and remorse; giving him the confidence to demand extraordinary fees, and racked chamber rent from his prisoners; or else, crowding them into holes, dungeons, and common-sides, designedly made more nasty, to terrify the prisoner, who, for preservation of his life, is thereby forced to part with his money; or, there to be devoured by famine and diseases. This makes him let his tap-houses at such prodigious rates, that, where poor people ought to have the best and cheapest, they have worst in quality, and smallest in quantity, at excessive prices. Also farming his beds to mere harpies, and his great key to such pieces of imperious cruelty, as are the worst of mankind . . . while the bloated patron himself, all the while, maintains his family in pride, and an imperious wife, or, perhaps, impudent mistress, in excess and luxury, with what he has unconscionably drained from the ruin of the unfortunate.

His complaint, like so many before, had no impact on the system and six years later, in 1702, there was again the familiar complaint of maltreatment. This time it was about abuses to prisoners held for debt who complained that the keeper deprived them of their allowance of beef and of money which was given to them quarterly. This was the second time that the debtors had complained of their treatment; after the first occasion they had been grossly abused and threatened by the keeper and the turnkeys. One of the latter was further accused of encouraging 'lewd women, shoplifters, pickpockets and common strumpets to come to the felons and lye there all night'. More specifically they complained that the charity beef that was allotted to them was managed by seven prisoners, one of them under sentence of death, under the supervision of the prison staff; and although the number of debtors was about one hundred, less than half the allotted amount of beef was shared out between them. The rest was presumably sold and the profits divided. Prisoners without money were taken to a room called 'Tangier' where they were stripped, beaten and abused in a very violent manner. When they received their charity money this was demanded from them as 'garnish'. In theory, this was money which was to be expended on the prisoners collectively; although, as the debtors' petition makes clear, they had to either surrender it voluntarily or have it taken away from them by force. If they refused, they would lose other possessions, again by force, such as bedding and their clothes of which they had already once been stripped.

Even those that managed to retain their money were not safe, as the underkeeper would release the professional felons from other parts of the prison into the debtors' quarters to pick their pockets or get the money by such means as they could.

On Sundays the debtors were not allowed to use the chapel because the space could be sold to sightseers curious to see the prisoners under sentence of death.

Despite such complaints little or nothing seems to have been done about successive keepers' behaviour, and ultimately it was only by forbidding the selling of offices that the appointment of more responsible individuals became possible and a stricter control exerted over them. From 1734 the keeper was appointed by the City and paid a wage of £200 per annum.

Even so, the opportunities for exploiting the system were not exhausted.

Whittington's Palace; its burning and rebuilding

From its medieval beginnings the history of the prison fabric itself seems to have been one of constant decay and repair. Slow payments from the royal purse, apparent indifference by the sheriffs and an unending neglect by successive generations of keepers to carry out repairs for which they had been made responsible, helped to create the 'most ouglie and lothsome prison' that Holinshed refers to. The frequent references to repairs being carried out simply underlines the extent of decay into which it had been allowed to decline, thus making escapes more frequent. In 1275 there seems to have been a mass break-out when nineteen prisoners got away successfully. More repairs were carried out but a decade later four men and a woman managed to break out, but only as far as the roof of the gatehouse where for a whole day they successfully resisted all attempts to bring them down. Punishment was swift. As soon as they were recaptured they were hanged.

The prison was broken into at the time of Tyler's rebellion but the extent of the damage that was done is not known. Conditions inside the prison were appalling. Out of eighty-five inquests entered on the Coroner's Roll for the years 1315-16, sixty-two were on prisoners in Newgate. Most prison deaths were attributable to gaol-fever, the modern typhus fever, which is highly infectious. It is characterized by a petechial rash and high temperature caused by infected lice, often found in the clothing or bedding, or rat fleas. So bad were these outbreaks that in 1378 City freemen, instead of being transferred from the compters, were imprisoned in Ludgate, except for cases of felony or maiming, so as to relieve them from the horrors of Newgate. Women seem to have suffered worse. They were kept in a small, overcrowded room; to get to a privy they had to struggle through the 'Bocardo' where some of the men were kept. It was not until 1406 that the sheriffs were granted a piece of land on the south side of the gate where they could build a stone tower for female prisoners only.

In June 1419 it was ordered that Ludgate should be abolished and the prisoners transferred to Newgate. Within four months the order had to be rescinded by the mayor, Richard Whittington, as so many prisoners had died who, as was candidly admitted, might have been living still had it not been for the 'fetid and corrupt atmosphere that is in the *heynouse* gaol of Newgate'. Some sixty-four persons, including the gaolers of both Newgate and Ludgate, died in this particular outbreak.

It was possibly this incident which persuaded Whittington to include a bequest in his will for the rebuilding of Newgate. Charitable bequests were not uncommon but not on such a munificent scale. Probably the most imaginative was that of a former mayor, Thomas Knolles, who had paid for water to be piped into the prison from the same cistern that was piping water into nearby St Bartholomew's hospital.

When Whittington died a few years later the royal permission was sought and given by Henry VI to pull down the gaol and rebuild a new one on the same site. This patent was signed on 12th May 1423. The new prison was nicknamed 'Whittington's Palace' or more simply 'The Whit'.

Certain distinctions were made in the new prison. A new feature was a hall where meals could be eaten; to the north were rooms where freemen were lodged and to the south, where the original tower had been built for women, the freewomen were housed. As citizens of London they had an obvious edge over outsiders who were put into less comfortable quarters; felons and prisoners awaiting trial on more serious charges were not allowed to mingle with them. Some were kept chained in underground rooms that are described as 'most stronge and derke'. Most prisoners, it seems, were kept chained at this time unless they could pay the keepers a surety against escape. It was, says one of the chroniclers, a 'soore streite and perillous prisone for any man to be yn'.

Gradually the stonework crumbled, the prison deteriorated, so much so, that, in February 1628, when a committee reported on the estimated costs of repairs they saw 'the ruins of Newgate' and found 'them to be many both in the stonework, leads and other things' and badly in need of repair. They estimated the repairs at over £500 and broke the costs down as follows: for carpenter's work, £45; plumber, £75; bricklayer, £50; mason's work and materials, £334 5s. Compare this with the bills of fifty years later when labourers were being hired for 2s 6d a day. Even allowing for a slightly higher wage for a skilled man it is obvious that £50 for a bricklayer was work for one man for a year. Another fact that the committee reported on was that the keeper, when he took office, had done so on the understanding that he would pay for the costs of such repairs. This is an insignificant footnote possibly, but one that perhaps shows just how much profit successive keepers thought that they could extract from the prisoners.

In 1662 the keeper was made liable for repairs except for the iron and stonework, which proved to be a useful loophole when the prison was destroyed in 1666. However, such costs seemed to have been successfully evaded by various keepers; they continued to be an issue until the keeper became a salaried officer in 1745.

The fire of 1666 destroyed most of medieval London, burning out the plague as it did so but left Newgate, badly damaged, still standing on the edge of the fire zone. In the plague of the preceding year more than 100,000 people had died; it had left the nobility and professional classes more or less unscathed but had swept unchecked through the poor and working classes who themselves had recognized how selective this virulence had been by referring to it themselves as the 'poore's Plague'. Nobody knows how many died in Newgate of the plague or that perennial hazard, gaol fever. No trials were held at the nearby Sessions House after June 1665. The Lord Mayor, alderman and judges had attended the customary opening of the sessions which were quickly brought to a halt when a prisoner, who was to be tried for blasphemy, shivered so uncontrollably when he was brought before the Bench that the judges, suspecting some other cause, sent for the master of the Pest-house to examine him. As the clothes were peeled away the tell-tale signs of the plague were exposed.

The abrupt cessation of the trials condemned many prisoners to an even lengthier confinement in a place where even at normal times the rate of fatality was high. One of the prisoners, a woman, was kept in until the next year for a 'felony valued at fourpence' while another woman, tried at the same sessions, had been released 'uppon baile' though charged with murder! One consequence of this abrupt cessation of the session was that it temporarily brought an end to public hangings. In the first six months of 1665, twenty-one people died on the gallows; from July through to the following February nobody was hanged. As soon as the plague had died down and the sessions resumed there seems to have been a feeling in the courts that a certain back-log had to be cleared; sixteen people were hanged within a month of the first hearings and a highwayman, for refusing to plead, was pressed to death.

After the fire what remained of the prison was so badly damaged that the remaining prisoners were led away under escort to the Clink, on the south side of the river, for better safe-keeping.

By 1673 Newgate was rebuilt. In appearance the gate was substantially the same one that had been built by Whittington's executors. This was a five-storey gateway, with a street running through a central arch which had cells in the rooms above it and in the supporting castellated towers on either side. Rebuilding work had cost about £10,000, a substantial part of which had gone on beautifying the gate with Tuscan pilasters, and large-scale statues symbolizing Peace, Security, Plenty and Liberty. The latter had a

Newgate prison in 1672. It was basically still Whittington's gateway, though heavily repaired following the Great Fire of 1666.

cat at her feet—supposedly an allusion to Whittington's cat—which one day fell down and was never replaced. Above the gates was a carved shield of the City's coat-of-arms. This exterior ornamentation, much of which could only have been a re-working of Whittington's prison, or that of his successors, brought criticism nonetheless that such beautifying was in sharp contrast to the ugly conditions inside.

The five-storey gate had cells in each tower. These were not very big, as the prison proper was in the annexes on either side of the street between them. In the centre part of the gate was an escape-proof room called 'The Castle'. Above this was the red room and the prisoners' chapel. These were the topmost rooms; above them were the leads where the prisoners were sometimes permitted to walk, if they paid a fee.

When prisoners were first brought into the prison they entered through a door, under the archway, which took them into the Lodge and from there to the 'Condemned Hold'. This was not a dark underground vault, as the name suggests, but had originally been a postern into the City. Let into the street wall was a tiny window covered with thick iron bars; this barely admitted any light, but prisoners, if they wished to lighten the gloom, could buy candles from the keeper. The walls and floors were of stone and the size of the room was about twenty feet by fourteen. Part of it was boarded over to make a sleeping area where you could only sleep, said one prisoner,

The London rairey Shows or who'll step into Ketch's theatre. *A satirical broadsheet published shortly before Sheppard's last escape; he can be seen behind the bars of the middle window. Jonathan Wild is sitting inside the base of the left-hand tower collecting viewing fees from spectators who have come to see Sheppard. Jack Ketch, with a noose and axe, is on the battlements.*

if your nose will suffer you to rest, from the Stench that diffuses its noisome Particles of bad air from every corner.

More intimidating were the chains, hooks and iron staples in the floor that were to bring unruly prisoners under control. The door, through which the prisoner had entered, was a heavy one with spikes at the top protecting an aperture through which the prisoner could speak to his friends, for eighteen pence, or negotiate for a better room with his gaoler. The anonymous author of *The History of the Press Yard*, published in 1717, says that the entrance fee for a better lodging was twenty guineas down and a weekly rent of eleven shillings; the keeper justified his prices by saying that he had had to buy his place for £5,000! His other charges included a cleaning woman (one shilling per week), a whore for the night (twelve pence), a visit from a friend (sixpence) or furniture which could be had for a minimal ten shillings rent every week.

Black Assize

For every person who was taken to Tyburn to be hanged in the early part of the eighteenth century generally four died in Newgate of gaol-fever or a related disease. Occasionally, as a result of the bad sanitation and over-crowding, an epidemic of disease would sweep through the prison and adjoining Sessions House, killing judges, prisoners, gaoler and spectators, turning a conventional sessions into a 'Black Assize'. One of the earliest mentions of such an assize was at Oxford, in 1577, when over 300 died.

In 1750 the gaol was more than unusually overcrowded. Parts of the army had been disbanded and, as commonly happened on such occasions, there had been a sharp increase in crime. According to a contemporary 'the very air they breathed acquired a pestilential degree of putrefaction. This contag-ion, brought by the foul cloaths and infected bodies of the criminals into the Court of the Old Bailey, at the Session in May, produced a pestilential fever amongst the audience.' More than sixty people died in the subsequent epidemic. Among those struck down were jurymen, barristers, the Lord Mayor, Under Sheriff and a former Lord Mayor. The prison had to be practically sterilized—in fact, washed down with vinegar. As an extra precaution the prisoners were similarly washed down with vinegar before they were brought to trial. In addition the judges, from that time on, carried with them and had on the bench before them a nosegay of flowers to ward off the prison smells. It is a custom which still persists.

Among the immediate plans for improving conditions in the gaol was one to knock down houses at the rear of the adjoining Sessions House yard and make a piazza where prisoners could exercise in the open air. A more practical step was the construction of a windmill on the roof of the gatehouse which it was hoped would draw off the poisonous air. The medical theory behind this was that stale air putrified and this in turn 'dissolves the blood and humours of human bodies' and set up further putrefaction which would ultimately dissolve the human body!

Several workmen engaged in connecting up the ventilation shafts to the prison's twenty-four wards became ill from the smell. Two years before, workmen at Bridewell had refused to carry out similar work for precisely that reason unless they were given tobacco and drink as precautionary measures; surprisingly they managed to stay immune but some carpenters working with them, who had not insisted on the same conditions, got gaol-fever from which two of them died.

The windmill seems to have had a limited success. The keeper was paid an extra £13 per annum to maintain it. A report was written on the first four months of its working. According to the writer's statistics only seven people had died in that period whereas in the same months of the six preceeding years there had been a total of ninety-nine deaths, making an average of sixteen deaths for that period, which meant in that first test period there had been a saving of nine lives.

The architect, George Dance the elder, was ordered to see what other improvements could be carried out. Consideration was given to buying up the older properties abutting the gaol with a view to opening up the cramped conditions of the prison. By the time that Dance had made his report the panic that had gripped the City fathers had died away and it was not until 1755 that the subject came up for consideration once more. Evidence was taken from various witnesses including the then keeper, Richard Akerman, who told the committee that part of the overcrowding was due to the fact that he did not use the upper storey as it was inconvenient for his servants; that the privies were often blocked and that the prisoners would not let the floors be washed as they argued that this would give them colds. Other evidence was taken from shopkeepers and inhabitants living near the gaol who complained that the smell was such that in hot weather people would walk past the prison holding their noses!

Dance's early plans were based on a reworking of the existing prison, enlarging it so that it could hold about 300 people. Akerman had told the committee that about thirty or more of the male prisoners were generally detained in one room and the women underground where the only light to be had was from candles. The committee envisaged the new prison as an 'airy' place where the prisoners would be able to exercise. After the public had voiced its complaints Dance received a fresh set of instructions and in July 1755 submitted a new design for a gaol costing about £25,000. It was to straddle both sides of the street, as before, only the gatehouse was to be rebuilt more as a triumphal arch with a main arch and two side arches for pedestrians, above which were to be placed statues of Justice and Industry. The estimated cost was £23,982. Other architects were asked to submit designs and there were suggestions that the prison should be rebuilt elsewhere. In February 1756 the committee decided to retain the existing site and was instructed by the Court of Common Council to obtain parliamentary approval for their plans. They never presented a petition seeking such approval, as preliminary discussions between the two sides indicated very clearly that Parliament would not vote any public money for such a scheme and that the costs would have to come from the City's own resources. Other suggested ways of raising this money fell through, and the whole question of rebuilding was shelved until 1764 when George Dance the younger took over from his father.

Gaol-fever

Despite the windmill and ventilator on the roof, prisoners continued to die of gaol-fever. Evidence too was now forthcoming that the sickness was not being confined to Newgate. Prisoners who were transferred to other gaols took the disease with them. The keeper's evidence was that between 1758 and 1765 eighty-three prisoners had died, besides wives who had visited their husbands, babies born in the prison and eight to ten of his own servants. Sixteen of this number had died in one month. His figures were further confirmed by the Middlesex coroner who, going back three more years (1755 to 1765), added an extra forty-nine deaths to the grim total. In his opinion all of them had died of gaol-fever.

Other statistics, which were not included, were of prisoners who had been sentenced to transportation but had died within a day or two of sailing. Some had died before their ships had even cleared the Thames. In March 1764 seven convicts were buried in Greenwich burying ground; their infected bodies had been cast out of the transport ship as she sailed and they had lain on the foreshore for some days.

Newgate burned

As the work of the committee slowed down it might almost have seemed that it did so in unison with the windmill, which seized up for longer and longer periods and eventually was not working on days even when a good wind was blowing. Discussions faltered, slowed down and finally stopped altogether as one by one the members of the committee dropped out. None of them knew what to do for the best; some had wanted the prison moved a little further west so that it stood alongside the Fleet ditch, no longer a creek for sailing-boats, but now an open sewer. Others thought such a move impractical as there was talk of a new north/south road which, if built, would cut through the proposed site.

Ultimately it was a further seven years of delays before the committee made its next positive step towards rebuilding. In the early hours of 7th September 1762 a fire broke out in the Press Yard and threatened to sweep through the gaol. The fire seems to have been started by one of the prisoners, a certain Captain Ogle, who had been tried for murdering a cook but subsequently certified insane and ordered to be detained during 'His Majesty's Pleasure'. Directly below his cell was another prisoner, Thomas Smith, a horse-dealer, who had been accused of stealing corn. Only the night before his wife had brought him about £500 in notes and bank bills.

The fire was too intense for the rescuers to get to them, and just before the floor collapsed Smith was seen to thrust an arm through the glowing bars and hurl his money to safety. Meanwhile, the other prisoners, terrified of burning alive, were shrieking for help. The keeper tried to calm them down by shouting that the fire was not in the main block where they were and, at great personal risk, had one of the turnkeys open one of the gates and let him in; calming the prisoners down he told them that he would stay with them and lead them to safety but in no way were they to try to break out and escape by storming the main gate. He then led the prisoners through a maze of corridors and locked doors until they were at the point furthest away from the fire. There he told them they would stay, and he with them, until either the fire was out or the guards came to take them to other prisons.

Escape, if it had been planned, had been foiled a little more easily than some other attempts that were made at about the same period. In June 1758 some felons, who were waiting to be transported, sawed through eight iron bars, each as thick as a man's wrist, before they were caught; the ringleaders were punished by being chained to the floor. In 1763 there was another attempt at a mass break-out; once again the prisoners had almost sawn through their chains before they were discovered.

In February 1764 the Prison Committee met once more, and after yet again discussing alternative sites, such as Ely Place or Aldersgate Street, decided that rebuilding would take place on the existing site. Dance proposed that the work should be a piecemeal redevelopment beginning with the debtor's quadrangle at the nearest end to the Sessions House, and once this was complete to move all the prisoners to the gatehouse and the extension to the north of it while everything in between was torn down.

Again there were delays, this time one of three years, until 1766 when Parliament gave its approval to the plans and passed the necessary Act so that work could begin. Even then the plans continued to stagnate while a new committee was formed. The elder Dance was made Surveyor and his son Assistant Surveyor. Fresh plans and estimates had to be made; but all this had taken its toll of the elder Dance and he resigned several months later because of ill-health, leaving his son to carry on with the work.

Until then the plans that had always been submitted had envisaged the prison straddling both sides of Newgate Street as it had done for centuries past. The gate was a growing cause of traffic congestion and so the younger Dance was given fresh instruction, that he was to re-design the plans so that the prison became a self-contained block on the site south of the existing gatehouse. For security reasons the great mass of stone facing outwards onto the street would be windowless and its only ornamentation some of the statuary from the old gate after its demolition.

In February 1768 Dance was given fresh instructions to look at the adjoining Sessions House which was in an equally dilapidated state. Parts of the fabric were cracked and in a dangerous condition. Dance estimated that it could be repaired but for practical reasons it was much too small for its purpose. He suggested that it should be rebuilt completely but as this was outside the committee's original terms of reference it was some months before this was agreed to. The final design that was agreed on was a prison block south of the existing gateway with a yard and wall connecting it to the Sessions House at the southern end.

At last rebuilding began, though there were still a number of unforseen delays, one of them due to the builder using the wrong sort of stone (Purbeck instead of Portland) and another due to a contractor getting into debt and finding himself for a short time in the prison that he was helping to rebuild! The first stone was 'officially' laid on 31st May 1770 by the Lord Mayor, William Beckford, though Dance himself was not present, being too ill to attend.

By 1774 the work on the Sessions House was completed. Next year two of the prison quadrangles were finished and the order was given for the gatehouse to be pulled down. It was sold for £150.

For the best part of 1,700 years there had been a gate on that site. Now it was just road.

The money that had already been raised by Act of Parliament was too little. The first complication was the unrealized depth of the old Roman ditch; because of it, an extra £19,000 had to be spent on putting in new foundations of nearly forty feet in depth. To raise the extra funds a second Act of Parliament had to be passed; £40,000 was raised, half of it being spent on completing the original design and part of the remainder going to pay for an infirmary which Dance proposed siting on a piece of ground near the condemned cells.

By June 1779 rebuilding was nearly complete. The final touches still to be completed were a covered passage for the judges and a piazza for a coach stand.

Despite its impressive appearance the prison was not without its critics. John Howard commented, but did not enlarge upon his words, that the new prison avoided many inconveniences of the old one but that it had some manifest errors which it was too late now to point out. He added ominously: 'All I will say, is, that without more than ordinary care, the prisoners in it will be in great danger of the gaol-fever.' In his review of the prison Howard visited the condemned cells. He described them, five cells on each of three floors, as being about nine feet high, with double-grated windows, doors four inches thick and stone walls covered by planks held in position by broad-headed nails. Each cell had a barrack bedstead. He was told by the warders that prisoners who had seemed indifferent or careless in court 'were struck with horror, and shed tears, when brought to these darksome solitary abodes'.

With the rebuilding of Newgate nearly complete the unthinkable happened.

On 2nd June 1780 rioting broke out in London. The spark that ignited this particular mob was Parliament's rejection of a petition from the Protestant Association—led by a fanatical anti-Catholic, Lord George Gordon—which demanded the repeal of the Catholic Relief Act, passed two years before.

Beneath the surface, however, bubbled in the demonstrators 'a groping desire to settle accounts with the rich, if only for a day, and to achieve some rough kind of social justice'.

Gordon riots

Angered by Parliament's refusal the mob took to the streets. To 'get the Papishes on the hop' they fired the chapel of the Sardinian Ambassador, which burned to the ground, and then ransacked a foreign chapel in St James'. Next day they attacked an Irish weavers' colony in Moorfields where they burned homes, and raped and attacked local Catholics for a further two days. Most of the City's constables and watchmen wore the white cockade of the Protestant Association and stood by, indifferent as to what was going on. They were encouraged in their attitude by that of the Lord Mayor (a former waiter and brothel keeper) whose only recorded comment was: 'The whole mischief seems to be that the mob have got hold of some people and some furniture they do not like and are burning them and what is the harm in that?'

In fact, there was no civil power to stop the mob. ('The civil power!' wrote the Rev Thomas Twining to Dr Burney. 'What is the civil power? A power that will be civil to a mob as the Lord Mayor was?') The watchmen disappeared from the streets; the army could not act without the sanction of the magistrates who, in the West End, were afraid to act through fear and, in the City, through favour with the mob. Emboldened by their success the mob seized control of the capital.

On Tuesday 6th June they gathered at Westminster to try once more to intimidate Parliament. Under pressure from George III a magistrate had been found who was ready to risk lynching by reading of the Riot Act—which alone would empower the military to use their muskets on the mob. Enraged by what had happened the mob burned down the magistrate's house the same night, together with the Bow Street offices where the 'Blind beak', John Fielding, brother to the novelist Henry Fielding, was magistrate and where he was continuing their pioneering work on police. From there the mob headed for the City.

The shout was 'Ahoy for Newgate!'

The Gordon riots: the burning of Newgate.

When an excited Henry Angelo ran to tell his friends that the mob was on its way to burn down Newgate he was laughed at for being so gullible. The new building was impregnable.

On reaching Newgate the first action of the mob was to seal off all approaches to it; they wanted to make sure that none of the prisoners could be smuggled out to other strongholds. Once this had been done they called on the keeper to surrender. Leaning out of an upstairs window he courteously refused to do so and then fled, taking his wife and children with him, over the roof as the windows of his Lodge were smashed in and his furniture dragged into the street and set on fire. Rioters began to batter at the prison gates and entrances with pick-axes and sledge-hammers, while others fetched ladders to climb the walls.

The keeper's house was soon on fire and became the main bonfire for the rioters' next objective, which was the burning of the prison itself. Before they got properly started there was a temporary interruption when about a hundred ward constables, who had been hastily got together, were marched up to the prison with the object of dispersing them. Acting on instructions from the ringleaders the mob opened up and let them through but once they were safely in, the trap closed up behind them; they beat them up and turned their truncheons into fire-brands which they hurled into the prison.

Swiftly the fire blazed its way to the prison chapel while more and more combustibles were heaped against the gates. One eye-witness wrote:

> The prison was, as I said, a remarkably strong building; but, determined to force it, they broke the gates with crows and other instruments, and climbed up the outside of the cell part, which joins the two great wings of the building where the felons were confined; and I stood where I plainly saw

their operations. They broke the roof, tore away the rafters, and having got ladders they descended. Not Orpheus himself had more courage or better luck; flames all around them, and a body of soldiers expected. They defied all oposition. The prisoners escaped. I stood and saw about twelve women and eight men ascend from their confinement to the open air, and they were conducted through the streets in their chains. Three of them were to be hanged on Friday. You have no conception of the phrensy of the multitude. This being done, and Akerman's house now a mere shell of brickwork, they kept a store of flame there for other purposes. It became red-hot and the doors and windows appeared like the entrance to so many volcanoes. With some difficulty they then fired the debtors' prison—broke the doors—and they too all made their escape.

Another eye-witness spoke of the wild shouts of the mob, the shrieks of the prisoners within expecting an instantaneous death from the flames or 'the thundering descent of huge pieces of buildings, the deafening clangor of red hot iron bars' and the loud triumphant shouts and yells of 'demoniac assailants'. Prisoners were dragged, shrieking and screaming, through burning rafters and walls, by their hair, arms and legs. Altogether about three hundred of them were brought to safety. In the surrounding streets witnesses spoke again and again of prisoners having their irons struck off by their rescuers and hobbling away into the eerie glow of nearby streets.

Still, the rioting continued. Having burned Newgate the mob moved off to attack the smaller prisons. Later that same night the flames from six different fires could be seen and from many miles away the flames from Newgate towered into the clouds and turned the night sky blood-red.

Thus was the strongest and most durable prison in England, in the building of which the nation had expended immense sums, demolished, the bare walls excepted, which were too thick and strong to yield to the force of the fire, in the space of a few hours.

Dance's prison

Next morning there was an emergency meeting of the Newgate Committee and an inspection was made of the ruins. The red-hot embers made a close examination impossible but workmen retrieved such re-usable materials as they could from what was left. Sightseers stood idly by as looters joined in the rescue work. Nobody interfered as about a hundred of them scrambled through the wrecked court-house. Among them were prisoners who had made no attempt to escape. These were easily recaptured and temporarily

housed in wooden cages (hastily erected around St Paul's) until the following year by which time the prison had been partly rebuilt.

Damage was estimated at more than £26,000. The shock at the prison's
destruction reverberated for many months.

> A massey building with an extensive front of rustic work, with all the
> appearance of strength and security. Yet, in the infamous riots of 1780, the
> felons confined, even in the strongest holds were released; stones of two and
> three tons in weight, to which the doors of their cells were fastened, were
> raised by that resistless species of crow, well known to house-breakers by the
> name of Pig's-foot. Such was the violence of the fire, that the great iron bars
> of the windows were eaten through, and the adjacent stone vitrified.

The riots were crushed by the army. The back of the riots was effectively
broken the next night when the mob tried to storm the Bank of England
and, despite repeated charges, and being led by a rider who waved above his
head some chains from Newgate, was beaten off with rifle fire and bayonet.
Considering the scale of destruction the official retribution was mild.
Sixty-two people were sentenced to death out of whom only twenty-five
were eventually hanged, one of them being convicted on the perjured
evidence of a professional thief-taker who, for some years, had 'lived by the
price of Blood'.

Someone considerably more fortunate was the then hangman, Edward
Dennis, or, as he was sometimes styled, the 'Yeoman of the Halter' or
'Finisher of the Law'; he was sentenced to death for having taken part in the
riots and helped with the destruction. Incredibly he petitioned the Court of
Aldermen from the death cell with a request that they should appoint his
son executioner in his stead; fortunately, he was reprieved but if he had not
been, and his request had been granted, it would have meant that the son
would have had to have hanged his father! Dennis' reprieve meant that
when he rode to Tyburn, it was not to die with his fellow-rioters, but to hang
them.

Londoners were appalled by the narrowness of their escape. While order
continued to be maintained at the point of a bayonet, talks began on the
need for reforming the police. To most people, until then, the word 'police'
had been associated with France and its repressive system of spies and
agents provocateurs; but in England the word was beginning to acquire its
more modern meaning of good public order and the prevention and detec-
tion of offences.

In the parliamentary debates that followed the word was used in reference
to the police at Westminster who were damned as 'wretched and miserable'.
Despite the wholesale condemnation that was heaped on their heads Parliament agreed to leave the system unchanged and continued to rely, as

*The Gordon riots: the hangman, Edward Dennis, who helped in the destruction and was
sentenced to death but reprieved.*

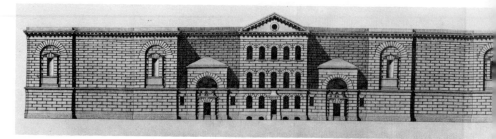

Newgate prison (1780).

before, on the army to suppress such 'guerres des pots de chambre'. In 1785 a police bill for London was thrown out while in the City itself a Day Police was formed the year before and the constables issued with a blue greatcoat to wear when they were on duty. Blue was chosen in preference to any more military styling as it was thought that it would lend them an air of distinction when they provided the prisoner's escort on execution day. From this macabre beginning the police uniform evolved.

As rebuilding got under way once more the opportunity was seized to make some slight adjustments to the original design. The roof was completed in copper and the pediment over the Keeper's Lodge was replaced by an attic; except for certain rooms the walls were not covered over with oak boarding but plastered instead from floor to ceiling with a mixture of lime and hair. (The latter was usually from cow hide and in one bizarre instance elsewhere gradually worked its way through the plaster so that it looked as though a head was coming through!)

Despite these modifications conditions once again deteriorated within the gaol as is evident from a petition dated 15th December 1789 from James Simpson, the former surgeon, to the Court of Aldermen. He had been the first surgeon to be elected to that office on a regular basis and said that when he began his duties 'there were 190 Men and 68 Women with the Itch (a disease which it is impossible to keep a crouded (sic) prison free from especially where many of the Prisoners have been *years* without a Shirt on) and for various reasons there were hardly any removals for almost a year so that there were at one time 975 felons and 134 in the Debtors side, full double the usual number'.

It had been an unusually severe winter and from the crowded state and 'the wretchedness and distresses of the Prisoners many of whom had been confined for years, the Gaol-Fever raged several times with uncommon violence and fatality . . .'. So extensive was it that at one time there were nearly 200 ill and, out of his own pocket, Simpson had hired assistants and provided medicine. As compensation the Court awarded him two freedoms to sell, each of which was worth about £25.

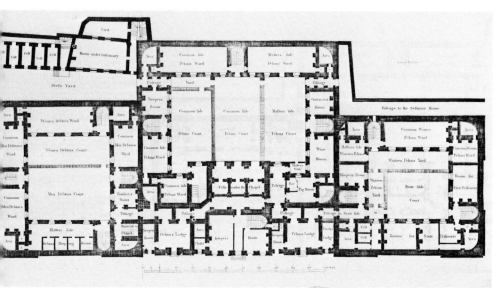

Ground plan of Newgate prison (1812).

Botany Bay

There is now but a step between us and eternity . . . the hangman and the scaffolding of the New Drop is already prepared for our executions on one hand . . . and military tyranny, at Botany Bay, awaits us on the other; we are accounted as sheep for the slaughter. . . .

> *The Prisoners' Petition to the Right Honourable Lord George Gordon, to preserve their Lives and Liberties, and prevent their Banishment to Botany Bay (1786)*

Among the early intake of prisoners was the inspiration of the 1780 riots, Lord George Gordon, who, so it was said, when he was first committed to the rebuilt prison, was confined in an underground cell the walls of which were covered with a green mould. This was exaggeration as, in Gordon's own words, he became one of the sights of London and entertained so many visitors in his cell that such was the overcrowding that it was impossible for everyone to sit down. Every fortnight he gave a dinner which was followed by music and dancing. He was tried for High Treason the following year but instead of being convicted, as everyone expected, he was acquitted as there was no direct evidence against him.

Sessions.	London.	Middlesex.	Hicks' Hall.	Weſtminſter.	Tower Seſſion.	Capital Reſpites.	Toli.
1723. January	10	19	3	6	-	-	38
February	8	24	9	-	-	-	41
April	16	24	19	14	-	20	93
May	10	29	14	-	-	-	53
July	14	49	6	5	-	-	74
September	11	24	9	-	-	-	44
October	10	17	8	6	-	-	41
December	10	15	9	-	-	17	51
	89	201	77	31	-	37	435
1774. January	4	18	3	-	-	-	25
February	16	33	7	3	1	-	60
April	15	24	17	13	1	-	70
May	6	22	2	-	-	-	30
July	14	22	12	8	4	30	90
September	22	16	10	-	2	1	51
October	8	8	6	5	1	-	28
December	14	22	16	-	1	13	66
	99	165	73	29	10	44	420
1775. January	9	29	14	9	-	-	61
February	9	20	7	-	2	-	38
April	19	17	12	4	-	-	52
May	5	9	2	-	-	-	16
July	6	11	7	5	-	20	49
September	14	20	6	-	-	-	40
October	9	10	7	4	2	-	32
December	8	9	7	-	1	11	36
	79	125	62	22	5	31	324
						Great Total	1179

Felons delivered from Newgate to be transported. (From Howard's The State of the Prisons in England and Wales.*)*

Over the next few years he searched for a new faith in which to be baptised; he became a Jewish convert in 1786, though he was denied burial in their cemetery, and significantly only after he had been rejected by the Quakers. Instead of being warned by his near-escape, Gordon began to court trouble once more. He became a regular visitor to Newgate, taking a special interest in those who were to be transported to Botany Bay, and it was on their behalf that he published a provocative pamphlet in which he libelled the judiciary. It seemed almost as if he wanted to be prosecuted. He was forbidden to distribute his pamphlet inside the prison and so had it distributed outside, provocatively sending copies to the keeper and the 'Ordinary' who, in private conversation, agreed with him that God's laws expressly forbidded the shedding of blood 'but he thought it was not his duty to tell the people who were dying that the laws of God were contrary to the laws they were going to be executed upon'. Gordon's uncomfortable answer to that was that he did not do his duty to God if he did not!

The prisoners who were being sent to Botany Bay had some justification for their fears. Once in the settlement they came under military rule; whatever abuses were committed, they had no right of redress, being denied judge, jury or counsel. This grievance was ignored by the authorities, who concentrated their fire on Gordon whose charges were construed as being 'calculated to incite insurrection, discontent and sedition' among the prisoners. He was charged with publishing two seditious libels (there was a second one on Marie Antoinette) but while on bail he escaped to Holland and was from there extradited, and after a short trial, sentenced to five

Transports going from Newgate to their embarkation point at Blackfriars (circa 1760).

years' imprisonment in Newgate. Even when he had served his sentence he was still considered too dangerous to be released; the authorities demanded that he find two sureties for his future good behaviour but no person was willing to take the risk. He continued to languish in Newgate and this cost him his life. Less than a year later he died of gaol-fever on 1st November 1793.

Parliamentary investigation

In Newgate the Prisoners herd together like Dogs in a Kennel basking in the Sun or prowling round and round the Yard, as I saw them; they appeared to be reduced as nearly as possible to the State of wild Animals inclosed in Cages. . . .

Evidence of W. A. Miles, Select Committee Report
on Gaols and Houses of Correction (1835)

In 1811 the House of Commons set up a committee to report on the laws relating to Penitentiary Houses. Giving evidence, the keeper, John Addison Newman, admitted his inability to control the prisoners. The gaol had been built to hold not more than 300 prisoners but, by filling every ward, infirmary and cell to its official capacity, this could be increased from a convenient number of 317 to 460; yet when the committee made its inspection the actual numbers were 900 felons and 300 debtors. Much of the overcrowding Newman blamed on the delays in shipping out the convicted transports to Australia who could be held up for twelve months or more. Even then some prisoners might be returned as being too ill or too weak to sail. Other grounds for the shippers refusing to take them were ruptures, bad legs, old age; and those who had no teeth were invariably returned. Others might be retained at Newgate if they had some particular skill, such as a carpenter, one of whom earned 5s. a week, or who had been nominated wardsman and proved particularly useful in maintaining order in his ward. Newman argued that if the transports could be removed and felons under sentence could be separated from the other prisoners it might be possible to find them work though, on his past experience, this was doubtful—an army contract for making scabbards had been taken away from the prisoners because of late deliveries and their stealing of materials.

Boredom was the prisoners' greatest enemy. Day and night they were cramped up in wards a regulation 15-foot wide but differing in length, the biggest being 38-foot long. The windows were barred and covered on the inside with wooden frames which had been papered over with greased paper

The Chapel Yard in the nineteenth century.

The Condemned Pew in the nineteenth century. Prisoners sat around the coffin.

to admit light and exclude air; the light that filtered through was so bad that they had to be opened. About six or seven feet from the floor were zig-zag ventilation holes in the walls, about six to eight inches wide, but these were often stuffed with rags to keep out draughts. Each room had a water closet and a fire. It was not uncommon for the prisoners to get drunk and the night before the Sessions began they would have a 'Free and Easy' and sing songs, generally obscene. The wardsmen would regularly smuggle in a bucket or two of ale for drinking after they had been locked up.

Visitors were allowed in but such was the lack of control that Newman admitted that it was not uncommon for them to have their pockets picked before they left the gaol. This was often done to buy more food, of which there was never enough among those depending on the charity of the sheriffs, who regularly sent in every week at their own expense 18 stone of beef. This never varied, however great the number of prisoners, which often meant that there was not enough to go round. The meat was made into a soup and doled out a ladleful at a time; if the soup ran out prisoners had to go hungry and take their turn, turn and turn about. On the women's side it was worse as some of them had as many as three children with them, from babies in arms to girls of 11 and 12 years old, though Newman was reluctant to let them come in as old as this.

The same overcrowding applied to the debtor's side. In 1813 it was officially supposed to hold only 100 persons but housed at that time 340 prisoners, 120 of whom were women when there was supposed to be only 60. The Corporation of London was not perturbed by such reports. Some years later, giving evidence to another committee, Alderman Sir Peter Laurie did 'not think any Man comes out of a Prison much worse than when he went in. I asked the Gaolers this Morning if they ever saw a Thief reformed, and they said they had not; and I never have seen one.' He believed in the silent system for instilling terror and was in tune with others who thought much as he did that prisoners had all they ought to have 'unless gentlemen thought they ought to be indulged with Turkish carpets'. Much the same philosophy pervaded the clergy, including an Archbishop who thought that prisons should be places of purgatory and not of paradise.

The treatment of debtors was probably one of the more iniquitous parts of the system. 'Costs were the gallons of sack to the pennyworth of debt' was another way of saying that the fees, which the debtors were often charged, far outweighed the debts that they had been imprisoned for and if not paid could delay their release. They could swiftly double or treble with the prison charges and the prisoner might never get free. The 1814 Committee condemned the practice:

> From every debtor . . . a fee is due to the Sheriff for his Writ of Liberate, amounting in Middlesex, to 4s 6d for the first action, and 2s 6d for every other: in London the demand is rather higher, and, beyond this, he may be further imprisoned until 6s 10d shall have been paid to the gaoler, and 3s to the turnkey: and your Committee indeed regret that any right should exist, by law, or by custom, of exacting fees from prisoners under these, or indeed, any circumstances. But, when the debtor's debt is paid, or when he has abandoned his property to his Creditor, and, destitute of every thing but his clothes and the instruments of his trade, looks forward to his liberty, it seems unreasonable that further demand should still be made on him, and

Newgate prison 1897. Taken at the corner of Newgate Street and Old Bailey.

that his liberation may yet be delayed until he shall have paid this new debt, arising only out of the satisfaction of all his former debts. That these fees have not always been extorted, nor made the subject of fresh imprisonments, is only to be attributed to charitable institutions, and to the humanity of the gaoler, whose right has never been enforced against the poor and unassisted. But your Committee feel that the character of the present gaoler is no security for the conduct of his successors, and that this power of oppression ought not to exist.

It was not until 1823 that feepaying was abolished and one can only assume that the committee was being deliberately disingenuous as, when the prison had been visited four years before, in 1810, some of the debtors had been detained for up to thirteen years for debts of no more than a few shillings. Among the cases recorded were those of a man and a woman who had been there for eleven years, the first for a debt of 1*s* 5*d*, and the second for a debt of 2*s* with costs of 6*s* 8*d*. Nor were these the worst cases. One man had been committed for the meagre sum of 4*d*, and, contemporary with these, but in the Coldbath Fields prison, was a boy who had been locked up for one month because he had not paid a 1*d*. toll and had no chance at all of paying the 40*s* fine which was subsequently imposed.

To ease the overcrowding a debtors prison was built in Whitecross Street on the north side of the City. This was completed in 1815 and one long-standing objective of the reformers had at last been achieved.

Newgate prison (1901) looking down Old Bailey from Ludgate Hill. The Central Criminal Court (the old Sessions House) is this side of the prison yard.

The Central Criminal Court (the old Sessions House) circa 1900.

Entrance to Birdcage Walk where prisoners were buried after execution (1902).

Newgate condemned

With regard to Newgate prison, its construction is such that it renders it totally impossible, even as a well-regulated prison, to do anything with it. It really is without a single qualification, but security from escape; it is a mere quarry of stone, without any order or convenience, or the possibility of establishing order within its walls. It is cut up into a variety of dark rooms, over which there is no inspection whatever; and though every attempt has been made, and the best advice has been taken on the subject, it has been found impossible to do anything with it with respect to its reconstruction.

Evidence of Captain W. J. Williams, Report of the Commissioners appointed to inquire into the existing state of the Corporation of the City of London (1854)

Under the Gaol Act of 1825 prisoners were supposed to be categorized, but Newgate continued to resist such changes. Other authorities, besides the Corporation of London, proved equally neglectful, a common complaint being their failure to provide statistical returns to the Home Office. In 1835 a Select Committee of the House of Lords, under the chairmanship of Lord John Russell, began an inquiry into the workings of the Act and the present state of the gaols and houses of correction in England and Wales. The City was a particular target, having resented such interference and having failed to implement the Act. It was possibly for this reason that in its first report the gaols singled out by name for particular criticism were those under the City's control—Newgate, the Giltspur Street Compter and the Borough Compter were said, in their present condition, to 'have the Effect of corrupting the Morals of their Inmates, and manifestly tend to the Extension rather than to the Suppression of Crime'.

The City's main witnesses were the keeper, William Wadham Cope, and Alderman Sir Peter Laurie who was very stiff-necked about the City's rights and privileges.

The trend in prison reform was to the separate and silent systems, the first system favouring the total isolation of prisoners and the second favouring not only the separation but silence, with no communication by word or look; in theory this would stop prisoners from contaminating one another and give them individually time for reflection. To this would be added strong discipline and work, usually meaningless, involving the treadmill or the crankwheel. Since 1818 there had been great improvements on the women's side of Newgate, where much-needed reforms had been carried out by Elizabeth Fry and her committee. Although she was convinced of the women's need to work, Elizabeth Fry wanted them to be taught how to wash, iron and mend rather than suffer meaninglessly on the treadmill. As a result of these principles being practised the number of women who had returned to Newgate on a secondary conviction had dropped by a third. In

Trial at the Central Criminal Court (1862).

Right: *Photographs taken of criminals sentenced at the Central Criminal Court (1869 to 1873). The length and date of sentence is at the bottom of each card.*

some respects, so she told the committee, she thought that there was more cruelty in the gaols than she had ever seen. The solitary system was a cruel punishment for children; this had been observed particularly in the vacancy of mind of girls 12 to 15 years old which in some cases bordered on insanity. Poor diet, hard labour and the system were literally crippling prisoners mentally and physically; in some places, where the prisoners were worked ten hours every day on the treadmill, they came out of prison permanently lamed.

Fortunately for the Newgate prisoners, the gaol's construction made classification and a silent system impossible without extensive rebuilding. Cope underlined this point by emphasizing that Newgate was a common gaol and not a house of correction. The minimum number in each ward was between twenty and thirty and some were there for less than one week. On

…4. George Stevenson
Clever Watch Thief
20 old
5ft 2 high
brown hair
hazel eyes
fair comp
3mo Thames P Ct
30th Sept 1870
other convictions

186 Mary Ann Welsh
Shop Thief
age 19
5ft 1¾ high
hair brown
eyes grey and weak
complex fair

18 Mo. C.C.C. July sess 1871

192 Louisa Roberts
Street Thief
age 25
5ft 6 high
hair dark
eyes blue
complex dark

18 Months C.C.C. Nov Sess 1871

79 Ann Spencer
Shop thief
18 old
4ft 9 high
dark hair
grey eyes
12mo C.C.C. Nov: 1869

No 94 Mary Jones
Street thief
32 old
5ft high
dark hair
hazel eyes
fresh comp
3mo C.C.C May 1871
other conviction

No 59 Chas Jackson
Shop thief
39 old
5ft 2 high
dark hair
hazel eyes
pale comp
15mo C.C.C. Nov: 1869

… Henry Hoyd
Office Thief
age 15
5ft 4 high
hair brown
eyes grey
complexion sale

Mo tts P. A. June 1872

115 Joseph Shephard
5ft Old Street Thief
38 old
hair brown
eyes blue
complex fresh

12 Mo C.C.C. Nov sess 1871

151 John Conner
Burglar
25 old
5ft 8 high
hair brown
eyes grey
complex fresh

2 Yrs C.C.C. July sess 1870
other convictions

AGES.	Males Committed.	Not Prosecuted.	Bill Ignored.	Acquitted.	Convicted of Minor Offence.	Convicted of Capital Offence.	Sentence Remitted.	Ordered for Execution.	Executed.	Females Committed.	Not Prosecuted.	Bill Ignored.	Acquitted.	Minor Offence.	Capital Offence.	Remitted.	Ordered.	Executed.
under 16	41	1	2	7	18	13	13	...	...	1	...	...	1	...	...	...	...	...
16	43	...	2	7	12	22	22	...	...	4	...	1	...	2	1	1	...	...
17	47	...	4	18	7	18	17	1	1	10	...	...	2	3	5	5	...	...
18	55	1	4	13	11	26	23	3	3	10	...	2	2	4	2	2	...	...
19	75	...	4	20	17	34	31	3	3	15	...	3	6	5	1	1	...	...
20	55	2	2	10	8	33	32	1	1	9	...	1	5	...	3	3	...	...
21	70	1	6	22	9	32	27	5	5	10	...	1	6	3	...	...	...	...
22	63	1	1	19	7	35	32	3	3	12	...	1	4	2	5	5	...	...
23	55	...	2	13	9	31	26	7	5	11	...	3	3	2	3	3	...	...
24	40	...	1	11	5	23	19	4	4	7	...	1	3	2	1	1	...	...
25	50	1	2	19	8	20	18	3	2	8	...	1	3	2	2	2	...	...
26	32	...	2	14	3	13	10	3	3	7	...	...	2	3	2	2	...	...
above 26	265	4	14	96	43	108	86	26	22	63	2	6	14	23	18	15	3	3
	891	11	46	269	157	408	356	59	52	167	2	20	51	51	43	40	3	3

The youngest person committed was a boy eight years of age, charged with stealing in a dwelling-house, and convicted of the minor offence.

An Account of the Commitment to Prison of Persons charged with Capital crimes, and of the punishment of death, in the County of Middlesex and the City of London, from 1 May 1827 to 30 April 1830 in the Order of the Dates of Commitment.

Saturday nights prisoners were brought in from Essex, Kent and Surrey for trial on the Monday morning. According to Laurie the gaol was more of a depot for prisoners to be held before their trial; since there were now twelve instead of eight sessions a year most prisoners were there a fortnight on average and certainly not longer than three weeks. Some were there for less than a week and after sentence were sent next day to one of the houses of correction. Transports seldom remained longer that two to three weeks.

Because of the failure in part of the Gaol Act, the committee was proposing a new Act. This would include in its provisions the right of the Home Secretary to appoint prison inspectors who would be able to visit every gaol, bridewell, house of correction and penitentiary in England and Wales and have the right to standardize procedures. In this way, some sort of control could be brought to bear on the penitentiary problems at a national rather than a local level. To achieve this would mean the local authorities surrendering some of their autonomy. This was anathema to Laurie who, as the City's spokesman, denounced the inspectors as spies, said that the City was hostile to them, that it was degrading to have them to see if you were doing your duty, that they would create dissatisfaction; he asked the committee to leave the implementation of the Act to the honour of the magistrates.

GENERAL STATISTICS OF NEWGATE JAIL FOR THE YEAR ENDING SEPT. 1860.

NUMBER OF PRISONERS.

	Males.		Females.
For trial at Assizes and Sessions...	907	...	208
Summary Convictions	—	...	—
Want of sureties	—	...	—
Remanded and discharged	148	...	69
Debtors and civil process	3	...	—
Mutiny Act	1	...	—
Tota commitments	**1059**	...	**277**

PREVIOUSLY COMMITTED TO ANY PRISON.

	Males.		Females.
Once	177	...	57
Twice	71	...	12
Thrice	24	...	2
Four times	10	...	4
Five times	2	...	—
Seven times, and above five	3	...	—
Ten times, and above seven	2	...	—
Above ten times	—	...	...
Total	**289**	...	**75**

AGE AND SEX.

	Males.		Females.
Under twelve years	9	...	6
Twelve to sixteen years	43	...	5
Sixteen to twenty-one years	206	...	59
Twenty-one to thirty ,,	434	...	101
Thirty to forty ,,	193	...	65
Forty to fifty ,,	113	...	33
Fifty to sixty ,,	34	...	5
Sixty and above	23	...	3
Age not mentioned	—	...	—
Total	**1055**	...	**277**

CASES OF SICKNESS.

	Males.		Females.
Greatest number at one time	18	...	5
Deaths	1	...	—
Infirmary cases	19	...	10
Slight indisposition	690	...	70
Insanity	—	...	—
Total	**725**	...	**85**

DEGREE OF INSTRUCTION.

	Males.		Females.
Neither read nor write	146	...	62
Read, or read and write imperfectly	607	...	185
Read and write well	293	...	30
Superior instruction	9	...	—
Instruction not ascertained	—	...	—
Total	**1055**	...	**277**

CAPACITY AND STATE OF THE PRISON.

	Males.		Females.
Constructed to contain	192	...	—
Greatest number at any one time	123	...	43
Daily average number in the year, male and female			92
Total	**315**	...	**135**

PUNISHMENTS FOR OFFENCES IN PRISON.

	Males.		Females.
Whipping	—	...	—
Irons or handcuffs	—	...	—
Solitary or dark cells	1	...	1
Stoppage of Diet	77	...	6
Other punishments	4	...	—
Total	**82**	...	**7**

ESTABLISHMENT OF OFFICERS.

	Males.		Females.
Governor and Deputy	2	...	—
Chaplain	1	...	—
Surgeon	1	...	—
Clerk and Schoolmaster	2	...	—
Schoolmistress	—	...	1
Upper warders' matron	2	...	1
Under warders	9	...	1
Other sub-officers	4	...	—
Total	**21**	...	**3**

General statistics of Newgate prison for the year ending September 1860.

His oratory had no effect; the new Act, which became law the following year, allowed for inspectors to be appointed, a uniform system of discipline, and rules and regulations to be approved by the Secretary of State. The committee recommended that there should be a silent system, before and after trial, even though they acknowledged that this might aggravate the severity of punishment, but shorter sentences should be allowed, which would leave a better chance of reform and, in their words, reduce the prisoners to 'inoffensive members of society'.

As far as Newgate was concerned they recommended that it should be reconstructed or rebuilt with a separate confinement of prisoners committed for trial. Russell had suggested five years before that it should be restricted to untried prisoners only, and that since they were being brought there from the counties outside London that half the costs should be borne by the public funds and that all convicted prisoners should be removed from Newgate. These proposals were submitted to the City once again, who agreed with them on condition that the management of the gaol was free from any interference other than that of the government inspectors.

Russell had hoped that a reconstructed Newgate might serve as a model on which the other prisons might be constructed or altered. The City wanted their costs limited to a specific sum but until there was agreement on the plans this was out of the question; from the early plans it was clear that any rebuilding would be severely restricted by the amount of land available. At the time when she was giving evidence to the 1818 Committee Mrs Fry had told them of a generous offer from the College of Physicians, whose premises backed onto Newgate, that they would disclaim any profit and sell the Corporation the building for use as a women's prison. They put their offer in writing but it was never accepted. In the Government's estimation a site of at least five acres would be needed, but even the purchase of an additional 50,000 square feet was thought to be not only too costly but insufficient for the purpose. They turned to alternative options outside the City and in particular to a piece of ground which the City had bought at Holloway to use as a cemetery. After further negotiations it was agreed that this should be the site for a new prison. Work was begun in 1849 and completed in 1852. It was modelled on the separate cell system at Pentonville with 438 separate cells for men and women serving short sentences.

Its completion meant that Newgate was now used for prisoners awaiting trial or who had been sentenced to death and that some long overdue rebuilding could take place.

The same architect who had designed Holloway was asked to prepare plans; single cells were to replace the wards which had existed until then. There were to be five floors of galleries with 150 single cells. Two would be for convicted murderers who were to hang.

The work was to be carried out piecemeal and involved the tearing-down of the north side, where the gate had once stood, and the destruction of the old press room, several wards and the condemned cells. The first stage was completed by 1859 but it was another two years before the female prisoners were temporarily moved to Holloway and the women's wing demolished. Work took another year and, when completed, added fifty-eight women's cells to the final total. According to the prison matron only about half of these were ever occupied.

Newgate demolished

We cannot close these remarks without an expression of the painful feelings with which we submit to your Lordship this picture of the existing state of Newgate. That in this vast metropolis, the centre of wealth, civilization, and information; distinguished as the seat of religion, worth, and philanthropy, where is to be found in operation every expedient by which Ignorance may be superseded by Knowledge, Idleness by Industry, and Suffering by Benevolence; that in the metropolis of this highly-favoured country, to which the eyes of other lands turn for example, a system of prison discipline such as that enforced in Newgate should be for a number of years in undisturbed operation, not only in contempt of religion and humanity, but in opposition to the recorded denunciations of authority, and in defiance of the express enactments of the law, is indeed a subject which cannot but impress every considerate mind with humiliation and sorrow. We trust, however, that the day is at hand when this stain will be removed from the character of the city of London, and when the first municipal authority of our land will be no longer subjected to the reproach of fostering an institution which outrages the rights and feelings of humanity, defeats the ends of justice, and disgraces the profession of a Christian country.

Select Committee Inquiry into the present state
of the several Gaols and Houses of Correction in
England and Wales (1835)

On Monday 26th February 1877 the whole building was threatened by a fire which broke out in the barristers' robing-room of the adjoining court and began to spread to other parts of the fabric. Workmen were carrying out repairs at the time, and it was subsequently thought that the fire had accidentally been started by one of the plumbers who, as soon as the alarm was raised at 1.50 p.m., hastily fitted up a hose-pipe and tried to stop the flames from spreading by damping down the ceiling over the Old Court Gallery. The Prison Governor and Chief Warder were hastily summoned to the Sessions House Yard where they organized a bucket chain until the fire brigade arrived. Despite their efforts the flames broke through the Old Court roof which collapsed and spread to a passage behind the Judge's bench where it was halted by firemen cutting away the heavy furniture and fittings. One of the other courts was saved by the cutting away of a ventilation shaft. Once the firemen had arrived the Governor was free to rescue the valuable law library, official books and documents as well as aldermanic and shrieval robes. By 4 p.m. the fire was out and the full extent of the damage could be assessed. Three of the courts were untouched but the fourth was badly damaged and the roof of the dining-room completely destroyed.

Under discussion that year was a parliamentary Act 'to amend the law relating to prisons in England' and which was aimed at bringing all prisons under government control; this became law on 12th July 1877. With the passing of this bill Newgate's days were numbered though it was to splutter fitfully on for another two decades. As from 31st December 1881 it ceased to

Central Criminal Court. Court Number 1 (circa *1900*).

exist as a prison and was only to be used as a temporary place of detention for prisoners awaiting trial or execution.

As the governing authority was now the Home Office and not the City, there followed a series of protracted discussions as to the prison's long-term future. At first it was thought that it was the Government's intention to pull it down but this was officially denied in January 1882. It was, however, ready to compromise on the size of the prison, which could be smaller, and settle the City's claims for compensation (the Act allowed the City to be compensated at the rate of £120 for every cell that was surplus to requirements) by conveying back to it the women's wing which the City could tear down and use to extend the Sessions House which it wanted to rebuild. The initial proposals had been rejected because they did not leave enough space between the two buildings.

The execution shed of Newgate prison (circa 1900).

The City accepted this offer, but there were further delays lasting seven years when new negotiations were begun so that the City could acquire the rest of the site for a greatly enlarged court-house. The Government stubbornly held out for a smaller prison but felt that the cost of the new court-house could be shared by the City and the surrounding counties which would come within the jurisdiction of the court. Overall control of the court would be retained by the City on the understanding that it would provide the site. New plans were drawn but like the earlier ones these too were found to be unsatisfactory. An added complication was that throughout these negotiations the Government was insistent that if a smaller prison was not built the City would have to find an alternative site or extra accommodation at Holloway. Casting about for an alternative site the City suggested the newly built Victoria Embankment; this was objected to as being too small. In despair the City picked up the negotiations on Newgate once more to see if there was a way of breaking this impasse and getting the Government to agree to surrendering the remainder of the prison still in its possession; either that or for it to shoulder some of the costs of the new court.

Eventually the Government negotiators agreed to surrender the rest of the site and withdrew its insistence that the City should provide alternative prison accommodation for the prisoners that would be displaced. Instead they would be placed at Brixton prison, but this would not be for another three years. Despite such a delay the Government agreed to part of the prison being torn down, though not at the Newgate Street end—which was in its possession and which was where the City wanted to start rebuilding so that it could keep the Sessions House in being until the change-over. The Government's final trump was to make the City buy back the male wing of the prison still under its control for £40,000 and to use the money for the extra accommodation at Brixton.

Plans for a Central Criminal Court to occupy the former site of the prison and Sessions House combined could now be drawn; the cost was fixed at £225,000. The Royal Institute of British Architects was asked to nominate six architects to submit designs. There was to be no restriction on style. All that was asked was that the new courts should have impressiveness and grandeur with not too much fussy decoration. The designs had to be submitted anonymously to a panel and were distinguished only by their allocated number from one to six. The choice was a difficult one and after eight months of consideration went to architect no. 4; this was E. W. Mountford.

Inside the execution shed. The gallows (circa *1900).*

Carrying out the gallows shortly before the prison was demolished.

The date for the handover was September 1901. The prison was closed and the demolition men moved in. On 15th August 1902 the first hole was breached in the outer wall of Newgate.

It was in the lowest block in the Old Bailey, the one nearest the Sessions House. Just beneath the Statue of Liberty, at a quarter past three o'clock, a piece of stone about the size of a foot fell out on the pavement, and a hand with a chisel in it was working away in the breach. A little crowd soon gathered to watch the operations. The old pigeons, rough and grimy as the prison itself compared with other flocks in London, fluttered about the statue, evidently talking over the event with much excitement. The doom of the jail was being carried out at last.

The Court

I am now come to the second Cause, which is the Treatment Felons receive after they are taken, both in Newgate and their Journey from thence to the Gallows . . . the Licentiousness of the Place is abominable, and there are no low Jests so filthy, no Maxims so destructive to good Manners, or Expressions so vile and prophane, but what are utter'd there with Applause, and repeated with Impunity. They eat and drink what they can purchase, every Body has Admittance to them, and they are debarr'd from nothing but going out. Their most serious Hours they spend in Mock Tryals, and instructing one another in cross Questions, to confound Witnesses; and all the Stratagems and Evasions that can be of Service, to elude the Charge that shall be made against them. . . .

Bernard Mandeville, An Enquiry into the Causes
of the Frequent Executions at Tyburn etc. (1725)

To keep out the foul air while in court, candied orange or lemon peel, preserved ginger, and garlic if not disagreeable, cardamom, carraway, or other comfits, may be very useful, and should the mouth be clammed, dry raisins, currants, or lemon drops, will cool, and quench thirst, which, should it increase, may be assuaged by small draughts of old hock and water, or small punch. Smelling to good wine vinegar during the trials, will not only refresh, but revive, more agreeably and coolly, than the use of spirituous waters distilled from lavender or rosemary, and more than any other scents.

Directions to prevent the contagion of the jail-distemper
commonly called the jail-fever. (London, 1772.)

Sessions House

When a gaol was 'delivered' it was cleared of the prisoners that were found there. Medieval gaol deliveries averaged twelve to sixteen a year; the committal could be as brief as three days and in exceptional circumstances up to two years. The Commissions of Oyer and Terminer (hear and determine) were more flexible as the defendants would not always have been in custody. The justices could order arrests, if necessary, and these would be carried out by the sheriffs on their directions or at the instigation of the Crown.

As the responsibility for bringing suspects to trial rested with the sheriffs, so too was it their responsibility that they should provide a Sessions House where the trials could take place. The earliest mention of a purpose-built Sessions House for the citizens of London and Middlesex is in 1334 when a hall and three chambers for that purpose were erected in Smithfield but for unknown reasons were allowed to fall into disuse. One possible reason might have been their close proximity to the live cattle market and the greater risk of disease. Whatever the reason the sheriffs continued a practice until Tudor times of hiring a suitable building on a yearly basis where the Sessions could take place. As the City lost its defensive character the great ditch that had protected it for so long was slowly filled in, despite orders to the contrary, and built over. In 1539 the Court of Aldermen agreed to the building of a Sessions House close to Newgate. Gaol-fever was obviously uppermost in their mind when they passed their resolution:

> Forasmoche as commonly prisons where Theefes and other malefactors be detigned for their offences be many times vysted with syknes and by reason thereof the place ys infectyd and moche peryll and daunger hathe chauncyd to the Justyces and other worshipful cominers attenying upon the Justyces for delyveraunce of the Kynges gaole: And forasmoche as there ys no cinveyent place wtyn this cytye for that purpose where the sayd delyverie shalbe made: And thes Cytye and Shryeffes of London for the time beying be greatly burdened for a conveyent place to be hyred yerely for the same; It is nowe agreed for the comfort of all thys Cytye that a conveyent place be made for that purpose holsomly to be orderyd and prepared upon the common grownde of thys Cytye yn the olde bayly of London wt all spede at the charged of the Chmbre of London.

The new Sessions House—its shape, size and appearance unknown—was built to the south of Newgate with a prison yard in between so that prisoners could be moved safely between the two. Like the prison at this time it stood outside the wall on what had formerly been the Roman v-shaped ditch. Because of its size and strength the wall was almost certainly the back wall of the prison yard. On this stretch of wall had been built in the thirteenth or fourteenth century two semi-circular towers or bastions, perhaps originally thirty to forty feet high. At least one of them was still standing in the eighteenth century and probably was not completely demolished until Dance's rebuilding. By the early eighteenth century it had lost much of its height, no major repairs had been carried out for 200 years or so, and it was almost certainly in a ruinous state with bushes growing out of its stone capping. It jutted forward into the Sessions House yard and cast its truncated shadow across the court itself.

Like its predecessor the Elizabethan purpose-built Sessions House was rarely used; again one must assume that gaol-fever was the reason why the justices preferred to sit in the open air, in a garden nearby, and take cover when it rained under a makeshift shelter. Like so much else of the City, the Sessions House was one of the casualties of the Great Fire (1666); a temporary court house of wood was erected and in use until 1673 by which time the new one of stone was completed. It was a conventional styled three-storey building with sash windows on the upper storeys and, on the ground floor, where the court sat, there were stone galleries for spectators where gentlemen could sit with their hats on, though the prisoners couldn't, and where they could gaze down at the forensic battles below them.

The Sessions House differed from its predecessors in one notable exception. Learning their lesson at last, the court, although it was under cover, was open to the air; there was no wall to the side facing the Sessions House yard. Prisoners could be brought direct from the gaol, shuffled into the bail dock—which had spiked rims to stop them from jumping over and escaping—and from there could be fed into the dock as and when necessary. There is only one recorded escape from the bail dock and that was of a highwayman who got away through the spectators but was later recaptured.

When the prisoners were brought to the bail dock, those who could pay 2s. 6d. to the gaoler were allowed to stand in the open away from the smells and infected bodies of the other prisoners who were herded below into the Hold, women on one side and men on the other, where they would stand like 'so many Sheep penn'd up in Smithfield on a Market Day'. The old hands took this chance to bully the other prisoners into paying 'Hold money' so that they could get themselves drunk before they were brought up to be tried.

Among the eighteenth-century turnkeys who had charge of the bail dock was a brutal individual named Spurling. Not only did he deal in stolen goods but his cruelty to the prisoners was such that they were eventually provoked into complaining of their hard usage to the Court of Aldermen. In September 1714, just as Spurling was ushering a coiner named Jane Houseden through the half door into the court dock, one of the other prisoners, William Johnson, tried to push through behind her. Spurling thrust him back and as he did so Johnson instantly retaliated by pulling out a pistol and killing him. At the same time the woman urged him on with shouts and cries. All this had been visible to the court and they were instantly sentenced

Sessions House circa 1675. The Roman bastion juts forward into the prison yard on the left hand side. The court is open to the air to limit the risk of disease. The entrance to the Bail dock is in the foreground.

An early eighteenth-century woodcut of a trial.

A more stylised version of the Sessions House. The bastion has been squared off and has trees either growing behind it or from it.

Right: *William Johnson shooting Mr Spurling, the head turnkey, while Jane Housden (then going to trial) stands by encouraging him (from Jackson's* New and Complete Newgate Calendar, *1818).*

to death. Neither of them seemed at all concerned by what had happened. Possibly they were satisfied that they had squared old grudges with the turnkey. On 19th September they were hanged in the Sessions House yard. Later Johnson's body was taken to Holloway and hung in chains with other rotting corpses.

As a precautionary measure and following on from what had happened, prisoners were kept outside in the bail dock—day and night—for the next eighteen months. That winter (1714/15) was a particularly hard one. It was so cold that the Thames froze over as far as London Bridge and fairs were held on the ice. It was known as 'The Time of the Hard Frost'. How the prisoners survived that winter without proper shelter or heat, or indeed whether any died, is not known.

In 1736 the Clerk of Works, who was then the elder Dance, was ordered to close up the ground floor with sashes, thus reverting to the original error of the previous two buildings and instantly increasing the risk of gaol-fever spreading to the court generally. This is in fact what happened; it led to the Black Assize of 1750, just fourteen years later, which struck down more than sixty people including jurymen and barristers as well as prisoners with whom the gaol was overcrowded and highly infected.

Gunpowder medicine

To guard the seat of justice from the approaches of infection, it will certainly be most prudent to fumigate and steam the place, by means of large braziers, pans, or coppers, put in the day before the sessions are to commence, and during that day to burn in them charcoal, with tobacco stalks, and dried aromatic herbs in winter, as mint, rosemary, southern-wood, etc., bruised juniper berries may also be burnt; and on a hot iron shovel may be put wet gunpowder, and frankincense, but particularly the steams of boiling hot vinegar should be conveyed to all parts of the building. The next morning about an hour or two before the court meet, the braziers should be filled with Coke Cinders, as used by maltsters instead of charcoal, and after they shall have burned a while, the ventilator should let in fresh air, and the floor should be sprinkled with cold vinegar of the sharpest sort. At the time of opening the court, the air-holes, made close to the ground, about a foot square, should be set open and the wooden flaps hooked up.

Directions to prevent the contagion of the jail-distemper
commonly called the jail-fever. London (1772)

After the Black Assizes the Sessions House was scraped clean and thoroughly washed with vinegar. Herbs were burned for several days at a time at the beginning of each sessions and thirty years of dirt was shifted from under the leads. To cut the risk of gaol-fever from ever again infecting court it was ruled that the number of prisoners that was brought at any one time to the bar to be sentenced was reduced from twenty to nine and that the bar was to be moved further back from the centre of the court to within a yard of the door. This was done so that any infection would theoretically blow away from court but possibly this was too impractical a step because the order was ignored and prisoners continued to stand in front of the judge's bench.

A more practical step, if it had been carried out, would have been to have followed the advice of the anonymous author of the pamphlet *Directions to prevent the contagion of the jail-distemper commonly called the jail-fever*, which was published a few years later. Not only was the prison a breeding ground for disease but so were the prisoners' dirty bodies and their equally dirty lice-ridden clothing. The anonymous author suggested that when prisoners were brought to trial that their clothes should be replaced with 'a long loose cloak, like a carter's frock, made of thick close Russia or other linnen on the outside, and lined with some sort of oilcloth, or glazed linnen, to be fastened close to the neck and wrists, and along the body, with hooks and eyes, covered over with a broad flap of the same linnen; and this cloak or frock made to reach down to their feet, so as to cover them closely, and entirely:

but no woollen, or heavy substance can be made use of, being well known to contract, and preserve infection. When the prisoners have no further occasion for these coverings, they may be washed, fumigated with brimstone, and afterwards wet with vinegar.' As an added precaution he suggested that all the time that the prisoners were in court tar should be burned in the yard!

The Press Yard

Although this was an exercise yard it was extended to include an apartment on each floor of the prison and was technically considered to be a part of the keeper's lodge which he could let out to the more affluent prisoners and where he could more easily milk them of their money. It was so-called because it was here that prisoners who refused to plead were put to the torture known as *peine forte et dure*, although torture in its other forms had been discontinued since 1640.

The object was not punishment, nor even to extract a confession, but simply to make the prisoners agree to be tried by a jury when they were brought before a court. As far as the law was concerned standing mute was not a confession of guilt and a prisoner could not be tried without his consent. He therefore had to be made to plead. The reason for such obstinacy, and why prisoners were prepared to risk this torture, and if need be die under it, was that if reasonably certain in their own minds that the evidence against them would lead to conviction, then in some cases their goods and property would be forfeit and their families left destitute and without means of support. By refusing to plead they could guarantee that this would not happen though their death might result. In the thirteenth century the law directed that such as did not plead should be put to hard imprisonment for having refused the common law of England.

Gradually the penalties became harsher. Prisoners were loaded with chains and fed a little stale bread one day and some stagnant water the next. Others were chained and left in the most appalling conditions 'barefooted, bare-headed and ungirt'. By the fifteenth century imprisonment was not enough. Prisoners had to suffer pain. One Lord Chief Justice directed that two suspects should be pressed with as much iron as they could bear and more. By Tudor times prisoners were placed between two tables and crushed beneath a load of stone and lead. Others had a sharp block placed under their backs so that the weight would break them. The judge's sentence was:

> He shall be sent back to the prison whence he came, and laid in some low, dark House, where he shall lie naked on the Earth, without any Litter,

Rushes, or other Clothing, and without any Raiment about him, save barely sufficient for decency: and he shall lie upon his Back with his Head covered, and his Feet, and one Arm shall be drawn to one Quarter of the House, with a Cord, and the other Arm to another Quarter; and, on the same Manner, let it be done with his Legs; and let there be laid upon his Body, Iron and Stone as much as he can bear, or more; and the next Day following, he shall have three Morsels of Barley Bread, without Drink, and the second Day, he shall have Drink three times, as much at each Time as he can drink of the Water next unto the Prison, except it be running Water, without any Bread: And this shall be his Diet till he die.

In 1658 Major Strangeways refused to plead when charged with the murder of his brother-in-law and he was ordered to be pressed. When he was stretched on the ground he was forbidden the piece of sharp-edged timber that would have guaranteed his back breaking under the pressure. The alternative was a wood door which was laid over him and on it were placed a number of weights. These were much too light and although he was in considerable agony he was able to sustain the pain. To hasten his end, and to guarantee that his property would not be forfeit, his friends, who were watching, added their own weight by standing on the door.

'The assistants laid on at first Weight, which, finding too light for a sudden Execution, many of those standing by, added their burdens to disburthen him of his pain. . . . In the space of eight or ten minutes at most, his unfettered Soul left her tortured Mansion, and he from that violent Paroxisme falls into the quiet sleep of Death.'

By an act of William and Mary, to encourage thief-taking, the law ruled that whoever captured a highwayman could keep his horse and furniture provided that it had not been stolen, in which circumstance it would have to be restored to its true owner. The highwayman William Spiggot refused to plead when he was tried in February 1721 unless his horse was returned to him. In the Press Yard weights of 350 lb were loaded on his chest but it was only when he had borne them for half an hour and a further 50 lb were added that he agreed to plead. He was tried, convicted and hanged. Another highwayman, Nathaniel Hawes, was broken in seven minutes with a much lower weight of 250 lb while another, Edward Burnworth, sustained weights of 424 lb for more than an hour before giving in, though he tried to end his sufferings by beating his head against the stone flags. Although this method of forcing a prisoner to plead was finally terminated in 1772, it was not until the nineteenth century that the court could enter a plea of 'Not Guilty' on behalf of the prisoner who insisted on staying mute.

The Press Yard (nineteenth century).

F. NASH.

Peine forte et dure, *the punishment inflicted on prisoners who refused to plead to an indictment (from Jackson's* New and Complete Newgate Calendar, *1818).*

Jack Ketch's Kitchen

The prison was divided into a 'common side' and a 'master side' with a combined total of eighteen wards, half and half, on the north and south sides of Newgate Street. The north annexe and gateway was exclusively common side with a number of those wards being Charity Wards for prisoners who could not pay the gaoler for better lodgings. These were sparsely furnished with bunks, hammocks, tables and sometimes a privy. Bread was brought into the prison each day and each prisoner was given or sold a round loaf. The only variation was on Thursdays when charity food was doled out. As the cook demanded 3*d.* per person for cooking it this meant that it often had to be eaten cold or raw.

According to the *Memoirs of the Right Villainous John Hall* (1708) the 'Cook Ruffian (that scalded the Devil in his feathers) comes to him for Three Pence for dressing the Charity Meat, which Charitably dispos'd Persons send in every *Thursday*, whereupon Earthen Dishes, Porringers, Pans, Wooden Spoons, and Cabbage Nets, are stirring about against Dinner time as thick as Burnt Brandy and Brimstone Possets in *Lucifer's* Kitchen, whilst the sweltered Cook sweats in Porriging the Prisoners, who stand round him like so many poor Scholars begging at the Kitchen Door for Colledge Broth. . . .' This was not to be confused with *Jack Ketch's Kitchen* where the public hangman 'in Pitch, Tar, and Oil, he boils the Quarters of those Traitors who deserve to suffer for the several Sorts of *High Treason*'. Another detail that Hall added to his description appertained to the Press Yard, where he described the heavy press of wood as being made like a 'Hog Trough, having a square post at each end, reaching up to the Ceiling, let up and down, full of Weights, by Ropes upon them, in which Torment he lyes Three or Four Days, or less Time, according as he is favour'd, having no Food nor Drink, but Black Bread, or the Channel Water which runs under the Gaol, if his fainting Pains should make him crave to Eat or Drink'.

The best rooms were in the south-east corner in a two-storey lodging adjoining the Keeper's Lodge and overlooking the Press Yard which in length was about fifty feet long by nine feet wide; one of the prisoners regularly exercised by walking an estimated four miles every morning before he went to breakfast. Some idea of the vast sums that could be made by the keeper can be gauged from his treatment of the Jacobite prisoners after the unsuccessful 1715 rebellion. According to the author of *The Secret History of the Rebels in Newgate* they paid out more money 'than would almost have paid the Rent of the best House in St James' Square, or Piccadilly, for several years'. A leading Jacobite paid sixty guineas for lodging in the keeper's house and another twenty-five guineas to keep off his irons! Others paid twenty guineas entrance fee and a sliding scale of charges from two guineas to ten shillings per man for every week's lodging.

Thomas Turlis, the hangman from 1752 to 1771.

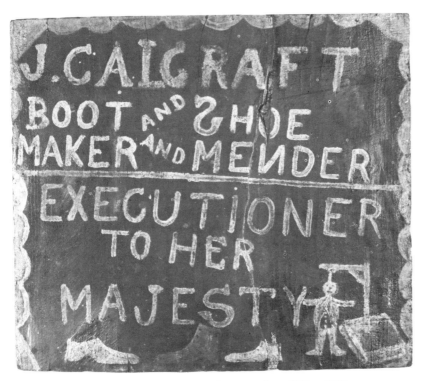

The shop sign of William Calcraft who was hangman from 1829 to 1874.

It was estimated that in the space of three to four months the keeper made nearly £4,000 besides the valuable presents that were given to him for other less well-publicized favours.

The Master Side

Each day began with the ringing of a bell at 7 a.m. and ended the same way at 9 p.m. when the turnkey on the Master Side, in Hall's words, hurried them up '(like so many Turkish Slaves) to their Kennels, which are join'd like so many Huts, as tho' they took their Order from Martial Discipline'. As those on the Masters Side had been committed on warrant and not yet brought to trial most of their time was apparently spent drinking in a candle-lit cellar and 'instead of holding Disputes in *Philosophy* and *Mathematics*, run altogether upon *Law*, for such as are committed for House breaking swear stoutly they can't be cast for *Burglary*, because the Fact was done in the Day time; such as are committed for stealing a Horse Cloath, or

Coachman's Cloak, swear they can't be cast for *Felony* and *Robbery*, because the Coach was standing still, not stopp'd; and such as steal before a Man's Face, swear they value not their Adversary, because they are out of the Reach of the *New Act* against Private Stealing. Thus, with an unparallel'd Impudence, every brazen faced Malefactor is harden'd in his Sin, because the *Law* can't touch his Life.'

In between times they slopped out, got breakfast (which they had to provide themselves) or wait until mid-afternoon when the prison meal was served; their loaf of bread might be supplemented from the sheriff's weekly delivery of meat or some charitable donation. Those on the Master Side usually had a roast or boiled joint of beef, lamb or mutton for their dinner. Those on the common side were generally eating below subsistence level, so much so that eventually keepers were forced to provide them with meat from their profits to keep them from starving.

The Common Side

Once locked up the prisoners were supposed to be asleep by ten o'clock but to enforce such a rule was clearly impossible. Some idea of the appalling conditions that existed in the Common Side can be gauged from a similar hold in another of the City's prisons, the Poultry Compter, which was also for debtors.

> When we first entered this Apartment, under the Title of the King's-Ward, the Mixture of Scents that arose from Mundungus-Tobacco, foul sweaty Toes, dirty Shirts, the shit Tub, stinking Breaths, and uncleanly Carcasses, poisoned our Nostrils far worse than a Southwark-ditch, a Tanner's-yard, or

a Tallow-chandler's Melting-room. The ill-looking Vermin, with long rusty Beards, swadled up in Rags, and their Heads some covered with thrumb Caps, and others thrust into the Tops of old Stockings; some quitted the Play they were before engaged in, and came hovering round us, like so many Canibals, with such devouring Countenances, as if a Man had been but a Morsel with them, all crying out Garnish, Garnish, as a Rabble in an Insurrection, crying Liberty, Liberty. We were forced to submit to the Doctrine of Non-Resistance, and comply with their Demands, which extended to the sum of two Shillings each. Having thus paid our Initiation Fees, we were bid welcome into the King's-Ward, and to all the Privileges and Immunities thereof. This Ceremony being ended, the lousy Assembly of Tatterdemalions, with their Fingers in their Necks returned to their Sports, and were as merry as so many Beggars in a Barn; some of them formed a High-Court-of Justice, by whom a Criminal was to be tried for cracking his Lice between his Teeth, and spitting out the bloody Skins about the Ward, to the great Nuisance of the good Subjects of England under confinement.

Garnish, similarly demanded of prisoners in Newgate, was levied on each inmate, so, in theory, the extra money could collectively benefit everyone by either supplementing the money that was given out of the various charities or by the buying of extras such as candles and other prisoners' comforts. In reality such money as the prisoner came in with was stripped from him, often by force, as soon as he was shuffled through the gate. According to Hall, as soon as a turnkey laid hold of a prisoner he would give three knocks as a signal to the 'Four Trunchion Officers', two of whom would hold him while the others searched his pockets 'claiming Six Pence as a Priviledge belonging to their office; then they turned him out to the *Convicts*, who hover about him (like so many Crows about a Piece of Carrion) for *Garnish*, which is Six Shillings and Eight Pence, which they from an Old Custom, claim by Prescription, Time out of Mind, for entering

The Condemned Hold in Newgate.

in the *Society,* otherwise they strip the poor Wretch, if he has not where-withal to pay it'.

There were other charges to pay but provided the prisoner could satisfy these demands and had money over then he could at least find a clean bed in the Middle Ward. The two worst places, in Hall's estimation, were the Lower Ward and an adjoining room called Tangier which was primarily for debtors. He describes the Lower Ward prisoners as lying 'upon ragged Blankets, amidst unutterable filth, trampling on the floor, the Lice crackling under their Feet make such a Noise as walking on Shells which are strew'd over Garden walks'. It was a 'real House of meagre Looks, and ill Smells; for Lice, Drink and Tobacco is all the Compound'.

From the end of the seventeeth century the prisoners were supposed to hold monthly meetings and elect their own steward and wardsmen; these were supposed to smooth out problems and help generally with the distribution of food and charitable bequests. The keepers cynically side-stepped these regulations and appointed their own favourites to these places. Complaints in the early part of the eighteenth century are numerous about them. They robbed corpses of their clothes and made relatives pay for the bodies before releasing them for burial. Prisoners who protested about their methods could be taken to 'a low Dungeon, hung all over with Spider Texture, and are there Shear'd, or put into Bilboes and Handcufft'; the sheers weighed about twenty pounds and, being rigid, when they were snapped about the ankles made it impossible to walk. Sometimes prisoners, particularly those that caused disturbances, were taken to the Press Yard and, so it is hinted, were 'pressed'. Goods were stolen, garnish money extorted and the prisoners financially raped.

Even when they had served their sentence prisoners could not always guarantee that they would be released. Perhaps Newgate's most famous prisoner in this context was Major Bernardi who, when James II was deposed in 1688, would not take the oath of allegiance to the new King, William III. Because of this he was arrested and thrown into Newgate to await his trial. No evidence was ever brought against him but both he and others were confined there for the next three reigns without ever being brought to trial. Efforts to get these men pardons were blocked and they were excluded from any amnesties. In 1722 there was a newspaper report which said: 'We hear that those unfortunate Men who have been 27 Years confined in Newgate by Act of Parliament, and exempted in all Acts of Indemnity since, are reduc'd to such Want, that they have Nothing to live upon, but the Common Allowance of the Prison, Bread and Water.'

A woman who had heard of Bernardi's distress not only married him but moved into Newgate with him and with her money moved him from the Common Side to lodgings in the Press Yard where she bore him ten children! When Bernardi died in 1736 he was eighty-two years old and had been in Newgate for more than forty years.

Sisters of the Night

Large numbers of children grew up inside the prison. Generally they belonged to families that could not bear to be split up and paid for the privilege of living inside the gaol. There was a constant risk, as one commentator said, of them being debauched by the inmates. Another related problem was the constant soliciting by whores and others on felony charges in the hope that someone could make them pregnant before they were brought to trial so that they could escape the rope by 'pleading their belly'.

According to Hall, the Women Felons' apartment on the Common Side was 'where there are a Troop of *Hell Cats* lying Head and Tail together, in a dismal, nasty, dark Room, having no Place to divert themselves but at the *Grate*, adjoining to the Foot Passage under *Newgate*, where Passengers may, with Admiration and Pity, hear them swear *Extempore*, being so shamefully vers'd, in that most odious Prophanations of Heaven, that Vollies of Oaths are discharg'd through their detestable Throats while asleep. And, if any of their Acquaintance gives them Money, then they jump into their Cellar to melt it, which is scarce so large as *Covent Garden* Cage, and the Stock therein not much exceeding those peddling Victuallers, who fetch their Drink in Tubs every Brewing Day.'

Children of such pregnancies were sometimes sent to the workhouses and others to the foundling hospitals. In the early part of the eighteenth century such women prisoners faced stern competition from their fellow 'sisters of the night' who some keepers admitted into the prison each night for purposes of prostitution. Some were even admitted into the condemned cells where the prisoners awaiting execution could spend the time that was left to them in drinking and whoring. Inevitably rumours of what was happening reached the Lord Mayor and Aldermen who were scandalized to hear that 'Lewd women and common strumpets' were allowed to 'lay there all night'.

In one instance a keeper who had been caught a second time tried to wriggle his way free by saying that these women were prisoners' wives, but his defence broke down when it was shown that one of them had slept with several prisoners in turn. The same keeper had encouraged these whores to let him 'fence' their stolen goods and had, in effect, used Newgate as a clearing house. He was dismissed, but it is probable, indeed almost certain, that similar practices were continued by his subordinates.

It was inevitable that such practices should continue while the City had little or no control over the offices that continued to be sold by public auction. It was this which led to the rise of the Thief-taker General, Jonathan Wild, and which caused the early eighteenth-century underworld to pivot on Newgate itself.

Thief-taker General

The head of the City's police force, its constables and watchmen, was the City Marshal together with his deputy, the Under Marshal. In 1696 both jobs were on auction for £800 and £300 respectively. Sixteen years later the price of the latter had more than doubled and was bought in 1712 by Charles Hitchen, a cabinet maker living in St Paul's Churchyard. He made no secret of the fact that he wanted the post for what he could make out of it. As he was deputy head of such law enforcement agencies as existed then, with his own marshalmen, and nominal control over the City's constables and watchmen, he was in a virtually unassailable position.

He concentrated on 'fencing' pocket books, private papers, bills of exchange and similar items which, although of no great value to the thief, were easily redeemable by the owner. Hitchen, in fact, would write anonymously to the victim, once the goods were in his possession, suggesting that if they wanted their return the loser should contact Mr Charles Hitchen in St Paul's Churchyard who was 'the greatest Proficient in the Business of Thief-taking in England' and warning them at the same time to come 'with your Pocketts well-lin'd, or he'll have nothing to say to you'.

Receivers, which is what Hitchen was, ran fairly high risks as the laws against receivers had been strengthened by two new Acts which had added branding, transportation and hanging to the other punishments of fining or whipping. Hitchen ran risks certainly, but because of his office he was in the unique position of being able to frighten off the opposition and dictate the prices at which he would buy. If the thieves would not agree to his terms then they generally found themselves threatened with prison and possible hanging, as one woman discovered when she was threatened with Bridewell. 'Unconscionable devil!' she complained, 'when he gets five or ten guineas not to bestow above five or ten shillings upon us unfortunate wretches.' Hitchen was not worried by such protests. He boasted quite openly that he had more than 2,000 thieves working for him, including a young gang of pickpockets whom he called his Mathematicians.

Although he was married, Hitchen was also homosexual and his interest in his young thieves was not entirely professional. He was a frequent visitor to Mother Clap's in Holborn and to a male brothel in Old Bailey. Once when Hitchen was seen at the latter fondling the young men who addressed him as 'madam' and 'ladyship' and who were 'hugging and kissing each other, and endeavouring to assume the most effeminate voices, telling each other that they ought to be whipped for not coming more frequently to school', he got into such a rage that he swore he would teach them a lesson. He promptly raided a house in Holborn where the men dressed in women's clothes and paraded them through the streets next day in those very garments.

They made such a ridiculous figure, that the whole street were in an uproar, for some of them had on gowns, petticoats, head cloaths, fine laced shoes, with all the other articles of female dress. Some had large hoops, others were dressed like shepherdesses, and some like raw country milkmaids.

Sentenced to hard labour the prisoners only got their release by sending Hitchen a letter threatening to accuse him of the same practices if he did not get them released.

Within eight months of his appointment the complaints against Hitchen were so vociferous, accusing him of blackmail, perjury, and receiving stolen goods, that he was suspended from office so that his accusers could prosecute him in the courts. The Lord Mayor and Aldermen could not intervene on their behalf because the office had been purchased; it was a nice technical point, and when his accusers failed to substantiate their charges in the courts Hitchen was able to resume his duties. He had been suspended for nearly one year and it was in this period that he had met and actively worked with possibly the greatest criminal genius that ever lived.

This was Jonathan Wild, in appearance a stocky man with a fierce animal courage and a strong instinct for survival. Four years of brutal confinement in one of the City's compters had hardened him. On his release he had set up as a receiver in direct competition to Hitchen and so successfully undercut him that the Under Marshal was forced to come to terms with him. In theory the two men were on opposite sides of the law; Hitchen proposed that Wild should become one of his marshalmen—unsworn, for the time being, as the Marshal was in disgrace—so that each would have a dual status as thief-taker and receiver. Their partnership lasted for little more than a year and when it ended did so in an acrimonious pamphlet war which did credit to neither. Hitchen's long-term satisfaction was to escort his former partner to the gallows. Wild never had the pleasure of seeing his old friend stand in the pillory which is where his vicious practices brought him.

After the break-up of their partnership Wild expanded his business by moving into bigger premises—the former Blue Boar tavern in Old Bailey, directly opposite the prison. From there he could keep a tight grip on the underworld. Apart from a small bodyguard he was independent of the London gangs. His methods were those of a professional businessman dealing with a number of companies, some of which were ripe for breaking up, others for merging into greater profitability; new alliances could be made, deals arranged and extra money be available for further investment.

Naturally there were casualties. Instead of producing redundancies and bankruptcies these particular mergers frequently ended in death. At the end of his career Wild tried to justify his methods by producing a list of more then seventy names that he had personally been responsible for sending to the gallows. This did not include the names of those who had been whipped, branded, transported to some foreign country or were still rotting in some loathsome gaol.

IONATHAN WILD THIEF-TAKER GENERAL OF GREAT BRITTAIN & IRELAND.

To all the Thieves,
Whores, Pick-pockets,
Family Fellons &c.
in Great Brittain & Ireland.
Gentlemen & Ladies.
You are hereby desir'd to
accompany ye worthy friend ye
Pious Mr I—— W—d from his
Seat at Whittingtons Colledge
to ye Tripple Tree, where he is
to make his last Exit
on   and his
Corps to be Carry'd from thence
to be decently Interr'd a=
mongst his Ancestors.

Pray bring this Ticket with you

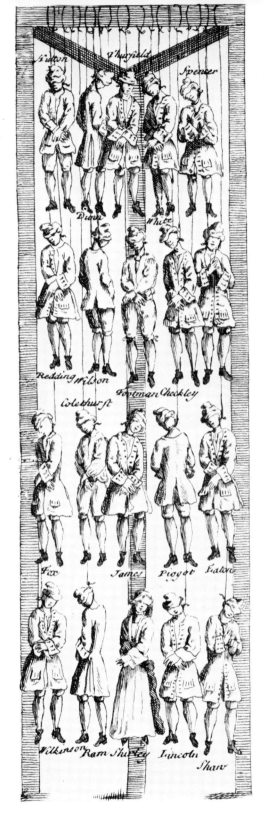

Funeral ticket to Jonathan Wild's execution. It asks for him to be accompanied from Whittington's College to the Triple Tree.

Some of Wild's victims hanging from the Triple Tree.

Inevitably numerous attempts were made at different times on his life. The last attempt was made shortly before Wild himself was brought to trial. He was walking among the prisoners in the bail dock, with a pint of wine in his hand, when he goaded one of the prisoners, Blueskin Blake, into catching him by the throat and trying to cut it with a blunt knife; had it not been for the several pleats of cravat tied about Wild's throat he would have succeeded. Blake subsequently swore 'with many bloody Oaths, that if he had murder'd him, he should have died with Satisfaction, and that his Intention was to have cut off his Head, and thrown it into the Sessions House Yard among the Rabble, and curs'd both his Hand and the Knife for not Executing it Effectually!'. Wild was still suffering from its effects when he himself was brought to trial. This was in addition to the accumulated scars, nineteen in all, which he had received in his gang wars; his skull had been fractured so many times that it was morticed together with silver plates!

Gangs twenty to fifty strong were wiped out by his organizational abilities. With his ledgers he could balance items which their owners had reported stolen against those self-same items that his thieves had taken on his instructions! Any discrepancies could be punished by arresting the thief! Against each thief's name Wild would enter a cross when he had enough evidence to hang him and when he did so he would add a second cross, thus originating the phrase 'double-cross'.

In a series of well-publicized arrests Wild became something of a celebrity and called himself in recognition of his own achievements 'Thief-taker General of Great Britain and Ireland'. As a paid professional police force did not exist, so society was forced to surrender more and more power to the hands of the professional thief-takers like himself. Hanging seemed to be society's only answer to crime. In the seventy years between 1690 and 1760 the number of capital indictments written down in law rose from under eighty to over three hundred and fifty. There was literally nothing for which a man could not be hanged. The new acts encouraged informers and professional thief-takers who would form 'Blood money conspiracies' to frame innocent persons with perjured evidence for the sake of the rewards that were being offered. Men such as Wild had enormous powers over persons detained in the prisons, which is why Wild established his headquarters opposite Newgate. A prisoner explained:

> He said the Thief-Catchers went every morning to all the Prisons, to seek for new Offenders; where they ask'd them their Case, and taught them how to plead; and if they had Money, would find some Contrivance, as in our Case, to bring them off; and whichever Thief-Catcher came first to such new Offender, he must be his Slave for ever after, and rob when he bid him, or be hang'd for refusing.

Jack Sheppard's escape

Occasionally somebody risked operating outside the system. In 1724 Wild was threatened with the resurrection of a gang that he had broken up the year before. The gang's new leader was a young locksmith named Jack Sheppard whose cockney impudence and two well-publicized escapes had already turned him into a national hero. Armed only with a razor and a chair-stretcher he had escaped from the St Giles round-house by breaking through the roof and scrambling down to the churchyard (which was two stories below) with only the help of a sheet and blanket tied together. Caught again some three months later he had made an even more dramatic escape from the New Prison, Clerkenwell, despite being loaded with fourteen pounds of chains. Not only had he cut himself free but he had released his mistress too; he had some difficulty in getting the overweight Edgeworth Bess through the cell bars after he had broken them but eventually did so when she removed her dress and petticoat. Even more remarkable, he lowered her twenty-five feet to the prison yard and then pulled her up an outer wall of the same height to freedom.

'Sheppard, not warned by this admonition, returns like a dog to his vomit', as one of the many pamphlets about him relates, and continued to haunt the neighbourhoods where he was known, cashing in on his notoriety to get new accomplices to help him with his burglaries and robberies. He was a singularly unattractive person to whom his escapes have given a certain glamour. He was particularly scathing of everyone that worked with him, blaming his way of life on his mistress and her 'wheedling demands for presents' and betraying almost everyone who helped him with his escapes without the slightest trace of remorse and with little or no pressure being put on him to name names. The appalling ease with which he was constantly recaptured was solely due to his own vanity and drunkenness.

One of Sheppard's accomplices had been Blueskin Blake. In July 1724 they broke into a draper's shop in the Strand where Jack had worked as a boy. His former master strongly suspected that he was implicated in the robbery and asked Jonathan Wild for help. Both men were swiftly arrested, tried and found guilty. Despite Sheppard pleading his youth and begging for the alternative of transportation, both men were sentenced to death. Sheppard was put in the Condemned Hold and immediately began making plans to escape. Executions were carried out on Fridays, and one week to the day that he was to die, and as some of the other prisoners were having their irons struck off and preparing for execution, Sheppard began sawing through his chains. The work took him the best part of three days but it was not until the Monday afternoon, with Edgeworth Bess and another woman to help him, that Sheppard broke free, prised open the spike and, heels first, slipped through to freedom. The women helped him into a woman's gown they had brought with them and, so disguised, Sheppard walked through the lodge and into the street where he picked up a coach at the corner of Old Bailey which took him to safety.

His escape created a fresh sensation. The turnkeys at Newgate were doubly embarrassed at his escape, as at the time that he was breaking out of the Condemned Hold at one end of the lodge they were at the other discussing what extra precautions needed to be taken to stop him from doing precisely that!

Sheppard again haunted the only area that he seems to have known well, about Drury Lane and the Strand. Not only was it a senseless flaunting of the authorities (he ate and drank in public) but an attempt to intimidate the very people that he had robbed and who had prosecuted him to conviction.

'The keepers of Newgate, (whom the rash world loaded with infamy, stigmatized and branded with the title of persons guilty of bribery, for conniving at his escape;) contributed their utmost to undeceive a wrong notioned people. Their diligence was indefatigable, sparing neither money nor time, night nor day, to bring him back to his deserved justice.' Eventually this 'Newgate cavalry', which was a posse of armed and mounted men led by the head turnkey, trapped him on Finchley Common. Sheppard was brought back to the Condemned Hold and in Newgate, according to the pamphleteers, there was nothing but smiles and bumpers 'in the lodge for many days together'.

Sheppard immediately began to plan a second escape from London's great gaol. His notoriety must have hindered his plans. He had a constant stream of visitors to see him. Fashionable London flocked to his cell. His gaolers were constantly searching him for tools of escape. On one occasion they found a file and on another a hammer and chisel hidden in the rushes of his chair. A popular saying of his was 'One file is worth all the bibles in the world'.

To make doubly sure that he could not escape the keeper moved him from the Condemned Hold, which was at street level, to a room called 'The Castle' which was above the gate arch. This was thought escape proof. To make escape even more impossible Sheppard was handcuffed and his irons locked and chained to a large staple fixed to the floor of his cell.

Sheppard carefully picked the time for his next escape. He waited until the turnkeys were busy with the Sessions, taking prisoners to and from the Sessions House. Wild was temporarily indisposed and nursing a partly cut throat; the words which had goaded Blake to his frenzy had been prompted by Wild's presence in the bail dock, where he had been coolly appraising the 'dead' value of each man, and his dismissal of Blake's plea that he should intercede for him with the words: 'I believe you must die. I'll send you a good Book or two, and provide you with a Coffin, and you shall not be anatomized'.

On 15th October, with about two-and-a-half hours of daylight left,

Jack Sheppard (1724).

Sheppard wriggled free of his handcuffs and using a bent nail managed to pick the great lock that was holding him to the giant staple before turning his attention to the chain that was holding his legs and which he worried, like a terrier a rat, until he had broken the weakest link and was free. He pulled his manacles and broken chains up to his knees and tied them into position while he considered his next move. The obvious way out was through the cell door, but there were prisoners on the other side of the corridor any one of whom might see and possibly hinder his escape. The other alternative was the chimney. He had already reconnoitred this possibility but the way was blocked by an iron bar set high up in the stack. Using his broken chains and the great padlock, which he had picked free, Sheppard began to attack the chimney breast. It was with great difficulty that he prised out his first brick but once this was done it became easier to widen the breach until he had finally torn in the chimney a hole about three foot wide and six feet from the floor. Only then was he able to wrench out the iron bar blocking his way. It now became a formidable weapon in his hands. Wielding it like a battering ram he tore an opening in the chimney breast up to ceiling level before breaking through into the room above, which he knew was empty. This was the Red Room and had been empty for nine years. The last prisoners it had held had been Jacobites brought there after the 1715 rebellion.

The door of this room had not been unlocked for the past seven years but in just as many minutes Sheppard had it open and was standing outside in the passage-way leading to the prisoners' chapel. The chapel door was bolted on the other side and for a few moments he was baffled as to how he was to get through. Using his iron bar he promply attacked the wall at the side of the door, eventually breaching it and making an opening through which he was able to pass his arm and push the bolt back. By then he had made so much noise that he was sure that he must have been heard by the other prisoners.

The chapel itself was broken up into a number of prisoners' pens each of which was rimmed with spikes. It was here that the prisoners heard the Ordinary's sermons and came to be gaped at by the public who paid an entrance fee for the privilege. Breaking through the entrance door of the condemned pew he found himself in the centre of the chapel and facing yet another partition. This time he ignored the door and climbed over, first kicking off a piece of the spike which he took with him as an extra tool. Descending some steps he was now confronted with the door opening on to the leads and which proved to be the strongest door that he had so far encountered. Worse, it was by now completely dark and he was forced to work without any kind of light. Using a nail, the spike and the iron bar, he attacked the box and after only half an hour's labour forced it away from its mountings. 'And so', he said, 'I made the humble door my servant.'

Six yards on he faced an even bigger obstacle. This door was guarded with more bolts, bars and locks than he had yet met with. As he was examining it the clock of St Sepulchre's struck eight which heartened him considerably when he realized just how much he had achieved in so short a time. The lock-box was fastened to the door with iron hoops; beneath it a stout bolt

The route of Sheppard's escape from Newgate on 15 October 1724.

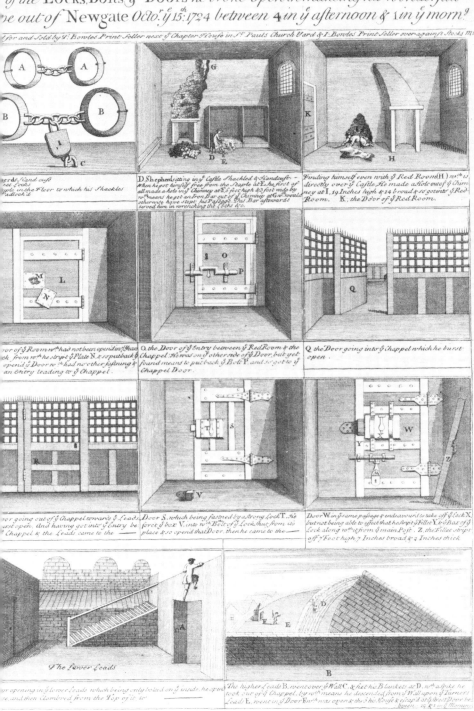

Exact Representation of ij Holes SHEPHERD made in ij Chimney of the Locks, Bolts & Doors he broke open in makeing his wonderfull ...e out of Newgate Octor. ij 15. 1724 between 4 in ij afternoon & 1 in ij morn.

was held in position by a clasp secured with a lock; an iron fillet seven feet high by seven inches broad and two inches thick was secured to the door frame with yet another lock. Sheppard, working in darkness, thought for a time that he had got as far as he could go. He continued to attack the lock but, realizing how hopeless this was, he turned his attention to the fillet. Using his iron bar he worked it below the clasp and with a tremendous surge of strength prised it away from the frame to burst the door open. As he ripped it away he brought the lock and the padlocked clasp with it. The last door leading to the leads was secured with a conventional bolt which was opened within seconds.

He was now in a walled area known as the Lower Leads. Standing on top of the last door, which he left ajar, he scrambled over the wall to the Upper Leads. Below him he could see rooftops and the street with its lighted shops. The drop was too great to the roofs below to risk with a single leap and so gambling on his luck, Sheppard turned back and returned to his original starting-point, the Castle, where he snatched up the blanket that he had been sleeping on. Fastening this to the Leads with his spike he lowered himself on to the nearest rooftop and scrambled to freedom through an open garret door.

Such an escape was without parallel and it was the sensation of the age. The court being in session, the keeper was instantly sent for and examined by the judges as to his security measures. Large numbers of people were taken on conducted tours of the escape route by the turnkeys who were anxious to assure everyone that the escape had taken place and that they had not connived at it. This was a smear which was widely believed and gaolers had a difficult time in convincing people otherwise. Because of the gaol's infamous reputation people were only too ready to believe that the gaolers wanted him free so 'that he should be at liberty to instruct and train up others in the method of house breaking, and replenish the town with new sets of rogues, to supply the places of those transported . . .'.

In the event, Sheppard's own folly caused him to be recaptured yet again. As before, he was drunk when caught. This time he was guarded much more strongly. He was loaded down with 300 pounds of chain, fastened to the floor, and guarded day and night. It was only after such precautions that he was brought to the gallows. Even then it was thought that he might cheat the gallows if he was resuscitated in time. When he was cut down a fierce fight began for his body. Being a light-weight he had suffered much when he was hanged. He had struggled for some time before being cut down after a quarter of an hour. Some of his gang tried a belated rescue, while other friends had a rented room nearby where they had a waiting surgeon ready to resuscitate him; but the mob, thinking that the body was being taken away for dissection, snatched it away and it was tossed over their heads out of his friends' reach. Eventually it was buried later that same night under the watchful eyes of a strong military guard.

Jacobite rebels

Let me exhort ye then to open the locks of your hearts with the nail of repentance; burst asunder the fetters of your beloved lust; mount the chimney of hope; take from thence the bar of good resolution; break through the stone wall of despair, and all the strong holds in the dark entry of the valley of the shadow of death; raise yourselves to the leads of divine meditation; fix the blanket of faith with the spike of the church; let yourselves down to the Turner's house of resignation, and descend the stairs of humility; so shall you come to the door of deliverance from the prison of iniquity, and escape the clutches of the old executioner the devil, who goes about like a roaring lion, seeking whom he may devour.

From a sermon contemporary to Sheppard's escape

Sheppard's escape was the most famous from Newgate though successive keepers were well aware of just how easily it could be done. Some years before the same keeper had had the experience of guarding Jacobite prisoners brought to London after the 1715 rebellion. Most were there awaiting trial. Although they generally maintained a high flow of spirits they were often quickly sobered by the executions of some of their fellow-prisoners. Some were hanged and others beheaded and quartered, which was the punishment for traitors. The head and quarters would be sent to different parts of the country to be fixed up in prominent places, generally above a town gate, as a warning to others. (In the late 1960s workmen were digging up the cross-roads at the corner of Old Bailey and Newgate Street when they turned up some skulls with the tell-tale holes in the cranium where the heads had been spiked above or near to Newgate. Not realizing their significance they threw them back into the hole as objects of no interest!)

Escape was always uppermost in the minds of these Jacobite prisoners despite the lavish treatment provided for them by their friends. According to an anonymous pamphleteer the prison had a carnival atmosphere and 'there was scarce any thing to be seen among them, but flaunting Apparel, Venison-Pasties, Hams, Chickens, and other costly Meats, with plenty of Wine'. On one occasion several prisoners brought a fiddler into the prison to play rebel songs but even the keeper drew a line at this and threw him out. Another day they had a badger brought into the Press Yard to be baited by dogs.

The first escape was attempted in March 1716. Some of them tried to break through the wall of the Press Yard but this attempt was foiled. Their anonymous pamphleteer brutally added that as a result some of them were 'put in Irons, to the Rust of which they added by their Tears, and the Water that came from the Knees of their Breeches'.

The next attempt didn't fail. One of the prisoners managed to get out of his irons and crept downstairs with them in his hands and placed himself by the door to the Condemned Hold. When it was opened he rushed out, knocked down the turnkey and with thirteen others bolted through the door into Newgate Street. Six were quickly recaptured and a seventh a few days later but the others got away. Security was strengthened, particularly in the Press Yard, and more rigorous searches made of the prisoners' visitors. Riding hoods and cloaks were found to conceal not only scarves but iron bars. One of the prisoners' servants made a wax impression of the outer door of the Keeper's Lodge and had a key made to fit it. Choosing his moment, he waited until his master and a friend were drinking with the keeper and, on the pretext that more wine was needed, went with the keeper's servant to the cellar to fetch some more. Ushering the keeper's servant in in front of him he locked the door behind him then waited by the outer door of the Lodge for his master to join him, which he did after a few minutes, leaving the friend drinking with the keeper. Using the false key they unlocked the outer door, which they relocked on the other side leaving the key in place so they couldn't easily be followed, and by next day were safely in France. The keeper was instantly arrested when their escape became known and was charged with High Treason, which carried the death penalty; he was suspected of being an accomplice but was fortunate enough to be acquitted.

In the meantime, a Lieutenant and thirty Foot Guards were stationed inside Newgate to prevent further escapes. A Catholic journeyman unwisely insulted them by calling them 'King George's bull dogs' and was shot. Still the escapes continued despite their presence. One Jacobite got out by the simple method of kicking his guard's feet from under him and running through the open gate. Another slipped under the chain at the gate with the help of an old rogue selling canes inside the gaol. The cynical comment was that money 'must be own'd the readiest Way to turn both Lock and Key'.

One escape which nearly came off was that of the prisoner who disguised himself as a woman, He made pads for his breasts and painted his face, as was the fashion, red and white. In spite of being close shaved and wearing women's clothes which had been smuggled in to him, the turnkey suspected him as soon as he tried to walk out with a party of ladies that had come to visit him and his friends. The ladies were part of the plot and as soon as the turnkey caught hold of him they began to abuse the turnkey and shout at his rough handling: 'Don't abuse the Lady, she's with child!'; and others 'Oh! my dear mother', at which the turnkey thinking that perhaps he had made a mistake hastily let go. The Jacobite would have got away had not one of the other turnkeys grabbed hold of him again and dragged him before the court, which was still sitting. He was ordered to be put into irons.

Understandably the dread that hung over these men during their confinement was the constant threat of the gallows and the headsman's axe which was the penalty for their treason. Some of the leading Jacobites had already paid the forfeit with their heads. Those that did die went to their deaths with the same sang-froid as did others some thirty years later after the second rebellion. The advice of one rebellious peer to another, when showing him how to position his head on the block, was 'not to wince, lest the stroke should cut his skull or shoulders, and (he) advised him to bite his lips'.

Dying confessions

Newgate is a dismal prison . . . a place of calamity . . . a habitation of misery, a confused chaos . . . a bottomless pit of violence, a Tower of Babel where all are speakers and no hearers. There is a mingling of the noble with ignoble, rich with the poor, wise with the ignorant, and the (innocent) with the worst malefactors. It is a grave of gentility, the banishment of courtesy, the poison of honour, the centre of infamy, the quintessence of disparagement, the confusion of wit.

Alexander Smith, A Complete History of the Lives of and Robberies of the most Notorious Highway-Men (1719)

Much of Wild's posthumous fame rests on the fact that he was a literary quarry for such contemporaries as Swift (*Blueskin's Ballad*), Gay (*The Beggar's Opera*), Defoe (*True and Genuine Account of the Life and Actions of the late Jonathan Wild; not made up out of Fiction and Fable, but taken from his own Mouth, and collected from Papers of his own Writing*) and Fielding (*The Life of Mr Jonathan Wild the Great*). Gay and Defoe were personally acquainted with Wild. In 1719 the former met Wild at the races at Windsor where Wild had 'discours'd' with great Freedom on his Profession, and set it in such a Light, that the poet imagin'd he might work up the incidents of it for the stage . . .'.

Nine years later *The Beggar's Opera* was a first night success. Wild had been dead three years but nobody had to guess at the model for Mr Peachum (Impeach them). Defoe's acquaintance was equally intimate. Not only did he know Wild, but as the reporter for *Applebee's Journal* (which had bought the rights in Sheppard's life) he had taken down the story at Sheppard's dictation while he was awaiting execution and may have been the person who had arranged for his funeral after the body had been yielded up by the mob. When Fielding came to write his satire he was fully conversant with Defoe's writings as well as the many other contemporary pamphlets on Wild.

Although using many of the facts of Wild's life, Fielding's story is primarily a novel satirizing contemporary politics and politicians, particularly the Prime Minister, Sir Robert Walpole, with parallels between the 'Great Man' and the 'Great Thief'. 'It was an effective device to suggest a parallel between the astute and corrupt thief and the astute and corrupt statesman, between the organizer of a gang for the pillage of the public and the organizer of a party for the plunder of the nations. . . .'

Newgate, in Fielding's hands, became an allegory. The debtors were the country's taxpayers ready to be plundered and its thieves the politicians planning to shear them. The struggle between Wild and his fictional rival, Roger Johnson, was that between the party leaders. The symbols of office are a silk nightgown, embroidered waistcoat and velvet cap. Gay's portrait of Wild as Peachum points the same message that he is intended to be taken as a portrait of Walpole. Swift underlined the point still further when he said: 'The author takes occasion of comparing those common robbers to robbers of the public, and their several stratagems of betraying, undermining, and hanging each other to the several arts of politicians in times of corruption.'

Satire was not the intention behind the 'Dying confessions' that were hawked about for sale on execution day. Most were straightforward pieces of journalism by reporters present at the trials. The best were generally written by the Ordinary or Chaplain of Newgate. As such he had unlimited access to prisoners awaiting trial or execution and he used this to advantage. Eventually they became an important source of revenue to him and, as such, had to be protected.

The 'dying confessions' were part of the ballad and chap-book sub-culture that began to flourish in the sixteenth century and which was to peak in the nineteenth. From single sheet productions these gradually expanded into pamphlets which were sometimes illustrated with a crude woodcut. The great source book for the Elizabethan and Jacobean dramatists was John Reynold's *The Triumph of Gods Revenge Against The Crying, and Execrable Sinne of (Wilful and premeditated) Murther*. In his preface the author says that he had purposely set these stories abroad, mostly in Spain or Italy, because it would grieve him to report and relate those that were committed in his own country. More ingenuously he adds that such stories might scandalize the subjects' friends and the author raise up enemies against himself!

No such scruples betrayed the Ordinary of Newgate. Initially his title was Visitor of Newgate and he was there to see to the spiritual needs of the prisoners. In the sixteenth century he was one of four chaplains of St Bartholomew's hospital, which was administered by the Mayor and Aldermen, who as the governing body of Newgate had him doubly under their control. He was instructed to 'visite all the poore and miserable captives', 'learne without booke the moste wholsome sentences of holie Scripture, that may comforte a desperate man', exclude 'brybes and all other corrupcion', encourage persons of substance to bestow some part of it 'to the relief of the nedy and diseased'; every quarter (at least) 'do such service in the saide churche as is requisite for such a Minister to do'; and the final admonition: 'This is your charge which see that ye do, and with any other thyng ye are not charged.'

The Visitor appointed in 1562 had not only such ministrations to perform but was somewhat bizarrely called upon to advise on the construction of a gallows! It was part of his duties to ride in the condemned cart with the prisoners to the place of execution, as did his successors, which may explain why his advice was sought on a cart to carry the condemned prisoners. His successor, Henry Goodcole, has been described as the first full-time chaplain of Newgate (1620-1641).His pamphlets may be considered as the fore-runners of what ultimately was to become the Newgate Calendar. Undoubtedly they had the right-sounding titles that would endear them to a crime-conscious public. They included *The Wonderfull discoverie of Elizabeth Sawyer, a Witch, late of Edmonton, her conviction and condemnation and Death; Heavens Speedy Hue and Cry sent after Lust and Murther; Natures Cruell Step-Dames: or Matchlesse Monsters of the Female Sex . . .; The Adultresses Funerall Day: in flaming, scorching, and consuming fire; or the burning downe to ashes of Alice Clarke late of Uxbridge . . . for the . . . poisoning of F. Clarke her husband. . . .*

Such pamphlets were an extremely important source of revenue to the Ordinary. Generally each pamphlet sold at between 3*d*. and 6*d*. From it the Ordinary might expect to make £25. As he might average out six pamphlets a year this would bring him in an additional £150. Just how profitable this was can be gauged from his official salary which was £35 a year and often in arrears; he was given two (later four) freedoms to sell which would sell for about £25 each; he had the use of a house (rent free) belonging to the City and a £6 bequest by the will of Lady Barnardiston. His official income therefore varied between £100 and £150 per annum, which could be doubled with the sale of half a dozen pamphlets.

Some were obviously more prolific than others, notably the Rev. Paul Lorrain, a Huguenot refugee and one-time clerk to the diarist Samuel Pepys, who became Ordinary in 1700. Lorrain published over 200 pamphlets and when a tax was levied on pamphlets he petitioned the House of Commons to be exempted by claiming that they contained 'nothing but Divinity, Devotion, and what may be most Useful to the World'. He explained that they contained the heads of his sermons, the substance of his admonitions to the prisoners and prayers for them and, almost as an after-thought, 'an Account of their Behaviour while under Sentence of Death, and their Confessions to him of what *Murders, Robberies, Thefts*, and other Injuries they have done to Mankind'. All this was done, he said, to prove useful to good men and to the wicked in 'plainly shewing them how to avoid an Untimely and Shameful Death in this World, and an Eternal one in the next . . .'

Interestingly, the anonymous author of *The History of the Press Yard* (probably Defoe) shows only too clearly what was in Lorrain's mind when he interviewed the prisoners. He narrates how Lorrain came to see a young man named Smith who was sentenced to hang. He began:

'''Well, Boy, now it's thy Turn to unbosome thyself to me: Thou hast

The CASE of
Paul Lorrain, Ordinary of *Newgate,*

Most humbly offer'd to the

Honourable Houfe of Commons.

HAT the faid *Paul Lorrain,* for the general Satisfaction of the Publick, the neceffary Information of Honeft People, and the Inftruction and Reformation of Wicked Perfons, does (after the Execution of Condemn'd Malefactors) ufually put out a Paper, containing the Heads of his Sermons, and the Subftance of his Admonitions to them, and Prayers for them; together with an Account of their Behaviour while under Sentence of Death, and their Confeffions to him of what *Murders, Robberies, Thefts,* and other Injuries they have done to Mankind.

That the faid 𝕳𝖊𝖆𝖉𝖘 𝖔𝖋 𝕾𝖊𝖗𝖒𝖔𝖓𝖘, and other Ghoftly Inftructions and Prayers, being Parts of 𝕯𝖎𝖛𝖎𝖓𝖎𝖙𝖞 and 𝕯𝖊𝖛𝖔𝖙𝖎𝖔𝖓, and thofe Malefactors Confeffions bringing Things to Light which were before buried in Darknefs, and are of great Ufe to be made known and publick: And both thofe 𝕯𝖎𝖛𝖎𝖓𝖊 Difcourfes of the faid Ordinary to them, and their Declarations to him, often proving Ufeful, not only to *Good Men,* in informing them in what they defire and have an Intereft to know; but alfo to the *Wicked,* in reforming them in what they are fo very defective, and making them fenfible of the Dangers and Miferies which attend a vicious and ill Courfe of Life; and plainly fhewing them how to avoid an Untimely and Shameful Death in this World, and an Eternal one in the next; and at laft to obtain the Favour of God, and the Life of the Bleffed:

The faid Paul Lorrain *moft humbly prays, That the Honourable* Houfe of Commons *would be pleas'd to Exempt from the* Tax *laid or to be laid upon all Single Sheets,* &c. *his faid Papers, which otherwife muft be difcontinued, tho' they contain nothing but* 𝕯𝖎𝖛𝖎𝖓𝖎= 𝖙𝖞, 𝕯𝖊𝖛𝖔𝖙𝖎𝖔𝖓, *and what may be moft Ufeful to the World, and is humbly conceiv'd were exempted by a late Act, a Copy of a certain Claufe wherein is hereunto annex'd.*

All which is moft humbly fubmitted to the Confideration of this Honourable Houfe by

Paul Lorrain, *Ordinary of* N.G.

A broadsheet pleading tax exemption for the 'dying confessions' written by Paul
Lorrain, the Ordinary of Newgate (1711).

been a great Sabbath breaker in thy Time, I warrant thee; the Neglect of going to Church regularly, has bought Thee under these unhappy Circumstances?'

'Not I, good Sir', replied Culprit, 'I have never neglected going to some Church or other, if I was in health, Morning and Evening, every Lord's day' . . .

'How, said Orthodox Sam, . . . no Sabbath breaker! Then thou hast been an abominable Drunkard, that is most certain?'

'Nor that neither', said the Youth. 'I was never given to that vice during the whole Course of my Life, having always had a mortal Aversion to strong Liquor from my Cradle, as my Friends tell me.'

'Sure the Boy's Mad, was the Question-monger's Return, I never had one Criminal under my Hands before, that was neither a Sabbath breaker, nor a Drunkard. Child, prithee recollect thyself, it will be better for thy Reputation after thou art dead, for the World to know that thou diest a Penitent.'

But he could extort nothing Satisfactory from the Lad upon that Head: Whereupon he took him to Task concerning another Article, and insinuated to him, That no doubt he had been a flagrant Whoremaster: He saw it in his very Countenance, which told him, That the Lust of the Flesh had gain'd the Predominance in him over his other Passions?

'You are under a Mistake there, also, good Mr Ordinary', was the Youngster's Answer, 'I have not known what a Woman is, carnally, to this Day, as I hope for Salvation in the World to come.'

With that, Sam began to be in a great Pet, and to cry out, Why the Devil's in this young Fellow, without all manner of question. He will neither own himself a Sabbath breaker, a Drunkard, nor a Whoremaster; the only three Topicks I can always enlarge upon, and yet has the Impudence to say, he hopes to be saved! Sirrah, you must be one of these three, that you must; therefore recollect yourself; set all your Faculties of Remembrance at work; or I shall be at a Loss to say any Thing of you in my paper.

'Then it's nothing with you to be a Thief', cry'd the Criminal, 'I am sure I find it otherwise for I am justly Condemn'd for so being.'

'Get you out of my sight', said his Reverence, 'such Case hardened Rogues as you would ruin the Sale of my Paper, I'll e'en write you down OBSTINATE;' and so he did: But others afterwards came in, and made him amends by more ample Confessions.'''

Each 'dying confession' followed more or less the same pattern. The pamphlet might begin by emphasizing its authenticity, as did the following, with the preamble: 'The Ordinary of Newgate His Account of the Behaviour, Confession, and Dying Words, of James Hall, Who was Executed at the end of Katherine Street in the STRAND, for the Barbarous MURDER of his Master JOHN PENNY, Esq.,' (1741). It begins with a résumé of the prisoners who were tried, the charges against them, date and place of trial, prisoners' pleas and sentences; this is about a page and a half.

Next comes the biography and an account of the murder together with several appendices, including Hall's own biography, claimed to have been written by him; the escape he contemplated which is written by another prisoner and several letters from Hall to a fellow-prisoner and his brother. Altogether the pamphlet makes about twenty pages including the title page (proclaiming that it is 'the fourth execution in the Mayoralty of the Rt Hon. Daniel Lambert Esq.', who was one of the victims of the Black Assize nine years later) and a half-page advertisement promising a full account of the five malefactors who were to be executed next day at Tyburn.

Most of the pamphlet would have been written by the Ordinary, with the possible exception of Hall's autobiography, the manuscript of which it was said could be examined at the printers. The only personal note struck by the Ordinary himself is to be found in the half page description 'At the Place of EXECUTION'. The Ordinary, who accompanied Hall, was James Guthrie, a former schoolteacher of Latin. Other Ordinarys included a failed poet and alcoholic among them. Guthrie says that when he came from the chapel he saw Hall's first wife sitting on a bench in the Press Yard. When she saw her husband she cried out and seemed to have a fit. She took off her hood, threw it on the ground and cried as if she'd been mad. Guthrie could offer little comfort; he could only advise her to submit to God's will. Next day he rode with Hall in the condemned cart. He includes the illuminating sentence that Hall devoutly complied with the prayers but added nothing more to his confession, which Guthrie had already given to the printer, and which suggests that even in those last minutes before he was hanged Hall was still being pressed for details. Guthrie ends his account by saying that just before Hall was turned off he cried to God to receive his soul. His body was allowed to dangle for three quarters of an hour before it was taken down and carried to Shepherd's Bush to be hung in chains.

What undoubtedly gave the Ordinary's account its uniqueness was the details that could be confirmed, denied or added to by the prisoner. Sometimes to get these details the Ordinary had to do an extraordinary amount of arm-twisting. Some prisoners would not co-operate with him, which is surprising when one considers the frequency and apparent readiness with which they were willing to betray one another. Sheppard is a classic example, betraying not only his mistress but the felon who helped him with his second escape. Both were punished for what they had done but at no time, judging from his published comments, does Sheppard seem to have felt any remorse at his betrayal. Possibly this readiness of betrayal is more understandable if one considers the number of offences that were punishable by death; betrayal might save them from that if not from imprisonment or transportation. This initial hostile attitude often changed after sentence. Some of the prisoners admit at this point that when they first came into the gaol they had thought to drag in a few more after them. Now they have accepted they are going to die they refuse to implicate others, arguing that to do so would only bring distress to other men's families. And it is at this point that they won't—some of them at least—co-operate with the Ordinary. They see no reason to have their own or other men's reputations publicly blasted and their families shamed by posthumous notoriety such as publication would bring.

Others were more relaxed and insisted on having their biographies written before execution so that they could have the pleasure of reading them. Undoubtedly some of them would have a good laugh at the Ordinary's expense—and the public's—by exaggerating and generally colouring their lives while dictating their memoirs, over several bottles, with their friends, and a whore or two, in their cell. Surprisingly, despite such exaggerations, there is generally a substantial skeleton of fact in such biographies which can be checked against the Sessions papers and other sources.

Others were anxious to sell their 'lives', and saw this as a way of defraying some of their prison and funeral costs as well as providing something for their families. There were plenty of people to urge them on. Some of them could sell their bodies to the surgeons for dissection. One man was overheard urging a prisoner to give him half a dozen pages of confession and in return he 'would tip him as handsome a coffin as a man need desire to set his arse in . . .'. This would not have been untypical of John Allen, who was Ordinary at the beginning of the eighteenth century. He ran a small funeral

Broadsheet for the trial of Henry Fauntleroy for forgery (1824).

THE TRIAL OF
MR. FAUNTLEROY,
The BANKER,

Aged 43, at the Old Bailey, this Morning, Saturday,

FOR FORGERY.

THE trial of this unfortunate man commenced this morning, at the Old Bailey, before Mr. Justice Park, and Mr. Justice Garrow. He was conducted into Court and placed at the bar, when he passed his eyes around him in a hurried manner, and his head then sunk down, conscious of the degraded state in which he stood. There were eight indictments against him, the whole of which were of the same nature,—for forging the signatures of several persons to warrants of attorney which authorized him to sell various sums of money from the Funds, and which were placed to his own private account at the Banking House of Stracey and Co of Berners-street, Oxford-street, of which he was a partner, thereby defrauding the different parties, and also the Bank of England. The first was for the sum of 46,000; the second, £17,500; the third, £10,000; the fourth, £5,000; the fifth, 5000l.; the sixth, 5000l. the seventh, 5000l and the eighth, 500l. making together 95,000l all of which was proved to have been received from the Bank of England, by the Clerks of that establishment. The evidence given was the same as have already been laid before the public in Mr. Fauntleroy's different examinations at Marlborough-street, and therefore deem it useless to repeat it. After a patient investigation, the Jury consulted a short time and returned a verdict of GUILTY.

LIFE, TRIAL, AND EXECUTION
OF JAMES GREENACRE,

With a Copy of a Letter addressed to Mrs. Greenacre in America.

INTERIOR OF THE   CHAPEL OF NEWGATE.

This man after a lengthened Trial, which lasted two days, viz, the 10th and 11th days of April, the particulars of which we gave in former publications, was found guilty of the Wilful Murder of Hannah Brown, to whom, as was supposed, he was to have been married

The only confession he made as can possibly be relied on, was as follows, though he had private communications with Mr. Cotton, and Mr. M'Murdo, the Chaplin and Surgeon of Newgate

When the Recorder had passed sentence upon Greenacre, he appeared to be very uneasy, and asked to see one of the turnkeys, he was accordingly waited on, when he stated, that when himself and Mrs. Brown entered his apartments in Carpenters Buildings, they had words concering the deception that had been resorted to, by both parties, when she being very agrievating, he took up a piece of wood, resembling a jack-towel-roller, and gave her a blow over the eye ; she was then in the act of falling, but caught her and placed her in a chair, then took a knife and run it across her throat, and placed a pail by her side to catch the blood. He then sat down to consider in what way he should dispose of the body ; many plans occured to him, but he decided on cutting it up, and disposing of it any way possible. He severed the head and legs from the trunk, and carried the head to Mrs Davis's in Bartholemew-close, (who in her evidence it will be remembered stated that Greenacre had a bag with what she supposed to be a quartern loaf in it), where he stoped until about 11 o'clock on the same evening as the deed was committed, (Christmas-eve), and then hastened on to

Stepney, and threw it in the Regent's canal, near the locks. He could then proceed no futher, but protested to the innocence of Gale.

LETTER.
Chapel Yard, Newgate,
April 30, 1837.

Dear Louisa,
I am sorry you should have to upbraid me with having forgotten the duties of a husband, but assure you from the hour I took my farewell of you, (which was then my intention to have b en but for a short period), through the treachery of those who termed themselves friends, I have been involved in difficulties, which has at length proved a fatal result, some idea of which you may form by noticing from whence this is directed.
There is no occasion, dear girl, for me to enter into the particulars concerning the cause of my lamentable end, as you will, if you have not already, through the medium of the press, which has, in every particular, endeavoured to blacken my character, undeservedly. However, I freely forgive all, as I hope to be forgiven, not only by man, but by my Almighty God, to whom, I hope, you will fervently pray on my behalf.

Receive, dear girl, the blessing of your ilfated and forlorn Husband,
JAMES GREENACRE.
P.S. Long ere this reaches you, I shall be no more.

EXECUTION.
This morning, at a very early hour, the houses facing, and all the avenues leading to the goal, were crowded with persons anxiously awaiting the fatal time which would assuredly terminate this wretched man's wicked career. At a quarter to 8 o'clock, the hangman appeared on the gallows, and prepared the rope, noose, &c. and at 8 o'clock, the Prisoner, attended by the Sheriff, and Chaplin, came forward in solemn procession, and was then shortly launched into eternity.

COPY OF VERSES.
All you who walk in follies path,
    Attention give to me,
And listen to the tale I tell
    Of my sad destiny!
In that genial pleasant month,
    When nature looks so gay,
I'm doom'd to die a wretched death
    On the second day of May.

Hard is my fate, for all will point
    With contempt and scorn,
Not one will heave a sigh for me
    Upon the fatal morn.
Must I die as a murderer,
    O, shocking is the thought,
To own a crime so very black,
    I never can be brought.

Thus spoke this wretched man, my friends,
    When he his sentence heard ;
He fears not God, he loves not truth,
    In all he acts absurd.
Then let us pray to God that we
    All deeds like this may shun,
And keep within a virtuous path,
    Til our race is run.

May all who ever acted wrong,
    Hence change their wretched plan,
Greenacre's case a warning prove
    To woman, child, and man.
All praise your God, and raise your voice,
    To shout his holy name,
Trust but in him, you need not fear
    You'll end your days in shame.

Broadsheet of the life, trial and execution of James Greenacre (1837).

Broadsheet of the life, trial, confession and execution of T.H. Hooker.

business on the side and used his position to pressurize prisoners and their families into buying items from him. His methods were complained of to the Court of Aldermen, particularly of the way he wrung money from them under the pretence of securing them bail or pardon. It is easy to see the powerful hold that the Ordinary had over prisoners at such a time. If they were awkward and refused to submit to his unjust demands he could shelter behind his cloth and tell them that they were damned and would go to hell. Since many of them would have been dying for quite trivial offences it is not difficult to guess at the genuine distress some of them must have laboured under in those last days between sentence and execution.

According to Wakefield, writing in the early nineteenth century, persons under sentence of death were engaged in a lottery 'of which the blanks are death'. Generally, at this time, there was a four-to-six-week delay (in Sheppard's time just over a week) between sentence and execution so that the delay of knowing who was to be reprieved and who was to die could prematurely age a man. Wakefield had known brown hair turn grey and grey white; as those under sentence of death sat apart in the condemned pew, grouped around an empty coffin, so the other prisoners would carefully note the tell-tale changes in appearance. In Wakefield's own experience, the smooth face of a man of twenty-five became wrinkled on the forehead and about the mouth and eyes; in three out of four cases this was generally accompanied by a great loss of weight.

'How thin he grows!' would be the whisper.

Neck verse

Have mercy upon me, O God, according to thy loving kindness: according unto the multitude of thy tender mercies blot out my transgressions.

Psalm 51, verse 1

Until the early eighteenth century, the by then anachronistic separation of the ecclesiastical and lay courts could still operate in the prisoners' favour; this was a medieval legacy whereby clerics would be tried by their own courts and as such could escape death by pleading Benefit of Clergy. Since literacy implied that he was a cleric, however humble, the proof was in his reading, or pretending to read, the first verse of Psalm 51 which became known as 'the neck verse' because it saved innumerable necks from hanging. The judge would ask 'Legit aut non legit?' ('Does he read or not?') and the Ordinary (from Chaplain-in-Ordinary) would answer 'Legit ut clericus' ('He reads like a clerk'). He could then be punished by whipping or fining but not by sentencing to death.

In time the whole practice became a meaningless nonsense as even illiterate rogues could be coached into remembering the one verse and, if not, either the keeper or the Ordinary would be willing to prompt them for a fee. By an Act of Henry VII Benefit of Clergy could only be pleaded once and the prisoner was branded on the ball of the left thumb ('glymmed in the paw') so that he could not make the same plea twice. Sometimes the mark was made in the palm of the hand, some judges wanting a hole through it!, while others more cynical or corrupt tolerated the use of a cold iron. For a short time, in the reign of William III, prisoners were burned in the face. The practice was discontinued in the reign of Queen Anne, but the metal skull caps which the gaolers used to fit on them to keep their heads steady were still retained as showpieces and used to extort 'garnish' from newly committed prisoners. Benefit of Clergy was abolished in 1827.

Prisoners were very much dependent on the forensic skills of either counsel, the magistrate or judge. From very early times they could not give evidence on their own behalf and any statements they made during the trial as a result of a searching cross-examination by their judge were not made on oath, as an oath implied some element of compulsion, and as such was inadmissible. By the end of the seventeenth century the practice of questioning prisoners had fell into disuse but prisoners could still make statements during the trial or have counsel make them on their behalf which became the more normal practice. Few prisoners could afford the costs of an expensive and well-prepared defence and the results for them were often disastrous. The following was published in 1833:

For several sessions I made a calculation of the average time which each trial occupied. I never found it exceed eight and a half minutes, notwithstanding many cases engage the court occasionally a whole day. . . . The average of eight minutes and a half is made on both the courts, and takes in all the prisoners tried for eight successive sessions. The rapidity with which the trials are despatched throws the prisoners into the utmost confusion. Fifty or sixty of them are kept in readiness in the dock under the court, to be brought up as they may be called for. These men, seeing their fellow-prisoners return tried and found guilty in a minute or two after having been taken up, become so alarmed and nervous, in consequence of losing all prospect of having a patient trial, that in their efforts at the moment to re-arrange their ideas, plan of defence, and put the strongest features of their cases before the court as speedily as possible, they lose all command over themselves, and are then, to use their own language, taken up to be knocked down like bullocks, unheard. Full two-thirds of the prisoners, on their return from their trials, cannot tell of any thing which has passed in the court, not even, very frequently, whether they have been tried.

This continued to 1848 when matters became worse still as the result of Sir John Jervis's Act, which laid down that the magistrate's examination was to be preceded by a warning that the prisoner's statement might be used in evidence and that he need not make one if he so wished. The result of this was that prisoners could not be questioned either before or during the trial!

Slowly the pendulum began to swing the other way. It was clear that if the prisoners' real defence was ever to be heard they had to give evidence on their behalf. The changes were slow to come about and the initial amendments to the law were in civil cases. It was not until 1898 that accused persons could give evidence on oath on their own behalf; they could not be compelled to give evidence. That it should coincide with the demise of the old gaol seems a little more that fortuitous.

Hanging judges

Possibly it was because prisoners were so poorly represented that judges intervened more frequently in the conduct of a trial. This inevitably led to them becoming more partisan than they should have been. The Stuart judges were particularly notorious in this respect, as was evidenced in the conflict between judge and jury at the trial of the Quaker, William Penn, the founder of Pennsylvania, and a fellow-Quaker, William Mead, at the Assizes of 1670.

They were charged with causing an unlawful and tumultuous assembly in Gracechurch Street and of preaching to the people assembled. They were refused a copy of the indictment and told that they would have to plead first. Both pleaded 'Not Guilty' and the court adjourned until two days later when the men were brought once more into the court. Quakers did not normally doff their hats to a court and when both men came into the court bare-headed, the Recorder, not wishing for the court to lose its fun, ordered one of the court officers to put on their hats again. The Recorder then asked why they did not show their respect to the King's Court and fined both men forty marks apiece for not removing their hats.

The evidence against the two men was slight; the Crown witnesses could only say that Penn was 'speaking' to the crowd, but as they could not hear what was said, there was no evidence that he was 'preaching'. The Recorder now began increasingly to take on the role of prosecutor and tried to trap them with his questioning. Mead protested: 'Doth not this show thy malice? Is this like unto a judge, that ought to be Counsel for the prisoner at the Bar?' When Penn tried to argue that they had broken no law the Recorder asked the Lord Mayor to intervene, to stop his mouth, and Penn was moved away, almost out of ear-shot, to the bail-dock. Technically he was still in court. Mead soon joined him, both protesting loudly, while the summing-up continued and the jury retired to consider their verdict. The two men were thrust into the 'stinking hole' below the bail dock. The jury returned after an hour and a half to explain that though eight of them were agreed on a verdict the other four were not. The bench immediately began to bully and bluster and dismissed them to reconsider their verdict. When they returned their verdict was 'Guilty of speaking in Gracechurch Street', which was nothing, and they resisted attempts to have the words 'unlawful' and 'tumultuous assembly' inserted into their verdict. They were ordered to reconsider again and this time they returned the same verdict in respect of Penn and acquitted Mead.

The Recorder ordered them to be locked up for the night without refreshment or other accommodation and told them: 'Gentlemen, you must be contented with your hard fate; let your patience overcome it, for the court is resolved to have a verdict, and that before you can be dismissed.'

Next morning, when the trial resumed at seven o'clock, the jury stubbornly held to its verdict. The mayor threatened to cut one of the juror's throats while the Recorder indirectly accused him of witchcraft! Again the jury was ordered to reconsider its verdict and just as stubbornly it returned the same one. When Penn protested at the continuing menacing of the jury the Mayor shouted: 'Stop his mouth! Gaoler, bring fetters, and stake him to the ground.' The Recorder added; 'Till now I never understood the reason of the policy and prudence of the Spaniards in suffering the Inquisition among them; and certainly it will never be well with us till something like unto the Spanish Inquisition be in England.' The Recorder continued to threaten the jury that he would starve a verdict out of them and that they should be carted about the City as in former times. He ordered them to be

Nineteenth-century plaster-of-Paris death masks taken after execution. The four smaller ones are from Newgate.

locked up for a second night and this time they acquitted both prisoners. The Recorder grudgingly accepted the verdict but fined the jury forty marks and ordered them to be imprisoned until this was paid. Prisoners and jury were all committed to Newgate but the legality of their imprisonment was challenged and by a majority of ten judges to two the independence of juries was upheld.

The conventional jury was twelve in number but when a foreigner was tried its composition was radically altered with sometimes quite unexpected results. Backstairs influence too could be brought to bear and a combining of the two could dramatically affect the outcome of a trial.

A glaring example of this was the trial of the seventeenth-century adventurer Count Konigsmarck for the murder of Thomas Thynne, who because of his great wealth was known as 'Tom of Ten Thousand'. Konigsmarck's three assassins are credited with the first shotgun murder in England and even more uniquely with having the moment of assassination carved on their victim's marble tomb in Westminster Abbey. The two men were rivals for the hand of a 14-year old heiress whom King Charles II wanted for his bastard son, the Duke of Monmouth. Money was the object of all three but it was Thynne, the ageing roue, whom the family agreed should have her. The bride fled immediately after the marriage, some accounts say 'before they were bedded', and Konigsmarck, thinking that she might marry him if her husband was dead, began to plot Thynne's murder. On 12th February 1682 three horsemen stopped Thynne's coach near Charing Cross and blasted him with a musketoon, five bullets entering his stomach and side. Konigsmarck had not been present and, when arrested, said nothing that would implicate himself in the killing. Part of the cross-examination was before the King and Council and Charles privately intimated that Konigsmarck 'might come off'.

On 28th February the four men were brought to trial. Largely through the skilful summing up of a pliant Lord Chief Justice the Count was acquitted; apparently the King was not displeased with the sentence although Thynne's friends were angry that he had been allowed to escape. The trial inevitably had its farcical moments. The prisoners were refused counsel, and as the only linguist among the defence counsel would admit to 'Pedlar's French', interpreters in Swedish, German and Polish had to be found; the interpreters could not understand all the languages involved and frequently found themselves acting as defence counsel. The judges would not wait for every question and answer to be translated but hurried the trial forward. The jury was half English, half foreign, because of the nationalities of the prisoners; they included two Swedes, one German and one Pole. Konigsmarck objected to Walloons being sworn as they were his country's enemies and made a similar objection to the Danes as his father had burned their towns! The case against the three who had done the actual killing was proved without too much difficulty; some extra evidence that was brought forward was thought unnecessary and dismissed as 'killing dead men'. All three were hanged.

For those who were familiar with the workings of the court this backstairs influence, particularly City influence, undoubtedly played some part in sentencing. Most of the documentation is nineteenth century. The court's governing body was the Lord Mayor and Aldermen, one of whom had to be present always on the bench. They, in turn, appointed the judges and in this closed circuit were undoubtedly able to influence many of the court's decisions either in mitigation or increased severity of sentence. Sometimes this influence was used to stop employees from getting a too early release which would let them pass on a firm's secrets to business rivals; instead of a light sentence they could receive a heavy one, such as transportation, which was out of all proportion to their offence.

One of the more glaring examples of how the system was worked was that of a cheesemonger's clerk who pleaded guilty to thirty-two cases of embezzlement, which was apparently normal when behind-the-scenes influence was at work. The most amazing aspect of this case was that the clerk had got not one but two people using their influence on his behalf; the prosecution were aware of this but as they had been told that he would be sentenced to two years' imprisonment, and not transported as had been likely, they did not dispute the arrangements. Incredibly, the second string had arranged a better deal and when the clerk was sentenced, instead of imprisonment for two years, he was fined the sum of one shilling which he had borrowed only moments before he stepped into the dock! Another instance was that of a shopman who stole marked money from his employer. In prison he was recognized by one of the turnkeys who had been a former servant of his father. The turnkey took an interest in his case and some days later told him that he had been able to get him off with a three-month sentence. In the same cell there were others, who for less serious offences were sentenced to seven and fourteen years imprisonment.

Sometimes the system worked the other way. The City was a close-knit, almost incestuous community, each ward having its Committee of Aldermen and Common Councilmen through which it could express its opinions. The most evil example of backstairs influence is told of Mary Jones in 1771 whose husband was press-ganged, leaving her and their two children, one a baby at the breast, destitute and with unpaid bills. Their few possessions were seized by creditors and the family turned onto the streets. In Ludgate

Number of convicts executed, for London and Middlesex, from 1771 to 1779 (from Howard's The State of the Prisons in England and Wales*).*

	Murder.		Coiners.		Various Crimes.		Total.
	Men.	Women.	Men.	Women.	Men.	Women.	
From Dec. 1771 to Dec. 1772,	3	–	2	–	32	–	37
Dec. 1772 to Dec. 1773,	1	1 burnt	1	–	29	–	32
Dec. 1773 to Dec. 1774,	–	1	–	–	31	–	32
Dec. 1774 to Dec. 1775,	1	1	3	–	40	1	46
Dec. 1775 to Dec. 1776,	6	–	8	–	24	–	38
Dec. 1776 to Dec. 1777,	2	–	1	–	29	–	32
Dec. 1777 to Dec. 1778,	1	–	1	–	31	–	33
Dec. 1778 to Dec. 1779,	–	–	2	1 burnt	19	1	23
	14	3	18	1	235	2	273

		Condemned.	Executed.	Pardoned &c.
Peace	1749	61	44	17
	1750	84	56	28
	1751	85	63	22
	1752	52	47	5
	1753	57	41	16
	1754	50	34	16
	1755	39	21	18
Peace & War	1756	—— 428 / 30	—— 306 / 13	—— 122 / 17
War	1757	37	26	11
	1758	32	20	12
	1759	15	6	9
	1760	14	10	4
	1761	22	17	5
	1762	25	15	10
War & Peace	1763	61 —— 236	32 —— 139	29 —— 97
Peace	1764	52	31	21
	1765	41	26	15
	1766	39	20	19
	1767	49	22	27
	1768	54	27	27
	1769	71	24	47
	1770	91	49	42
	1771	60	34	26
		—— 457	—— 233	—— 224
		1121	678	443

Abstract of criminals condemned, executed and pardoned at the Old Bailey Sessions House from 1749 to 1771 inclusive (from Howard's The State of the Prisons in England and Wales*).*

Hill, close to the Sessions House, she made a half-hearted attempt to steal some muslin worth £5 10*s*. but was caught in the act. There had been a number of similar such cases in the area and because of the shopkeepers' complaints the judges were determined to make examples of those caught. As the judge replied to the prisoner who complained that he was being hanged for stealing a horse, he was not being hanged for stealing a horse; he was being hanged so that horses would not be stolen. The same philosophy prevailed in this instance. Despite pleas for clemency Mary Jones was sentenced to death. When the condemned cart set out for Tyburn she was still suckling the youngest at her breast. She was not 19 years old. When her case was related to the House of Commons some years later, in the opinion of Sir William Meredith: 'Take all the circumstances together, I do not believe a fouler murder was ever committed against the law, than the murder of this woman by law.'

Transportation

Some idea of the numbers and sentencing that passed through the Sessions annually can be gauged from a report on the State of the Gaol of Newgate which was dated 28th September 1788 to 28th September 1789. Out of a total of 2,467 prisoners seventeen were executed, of whom one was burned, one dissected and one hung in chains, 826 were tried of which 301 were acquitted, 80 sentenced to death, 285 sentenced to transportation, 67 to be whipped, 91 sentenced to imprisonment, branding and fines, 2 fined and discharged.

The final breakdown, including some of the above figures, was as follows:

Of which were tried	826
Executed	17
Died	73
Removed to other prisons	41
Transported	270
Discharged	675
Remanded under sentence of death	20
Remanded under sentence of death but respited	9
Under sentence of transportation	434
Fines	66
In trial	36 *Total 2,467*

The interesting comparison is between those transported or waiting to be transported and those discharged; the figures are almost identical and together make up more than half of the final total. The practice of transporting men and women had begun in the early seventeenth century as an alternative to executing them; it soon grew into an extremely profitable business for the contractors who shipped them out to the plantations in the American and West Indian colonies where they went to serve their sentences. Labour was much needed and these 'servants' were bound to serve their masters for a minimum period of five years; James II had the Governors increase this to ten years. When they reached the colonies the prisoners were put up for auction and sold to the highest bidder; the price seems to have averaged between £10 and £15.

The prisoners had no rights, received no wages, could own no property, were beaten and flogged and if they survived their term they could be released with a token sum of money which, in the case of Barbados, was about 500 pounds of sugar—the equivalent of £5. This could be reduced by any fines they had incurred and acts of disobedience could actually mean an increase in sentence. Life was tougher for the whites who were called and treated as slaves the same as the blacks; the reason why it was tougher was because the blacks were being paced for a life sentence and the whites were not.

The American Revolution ended transportation to the Americas, but by then the alternative dumping-ground of Australia had been found, in particular Botany Bay—so-called because of the richness of its plants. The Bay's discoverer, Captain Cook, thought it would be a 'suitable destination for the savages at present a heavy charge upon their Lordships at home'. Six convict ships set out for Australia in 1787. The last one left in 1867.

According to an anonymous chronicler writing in the early nineteenth century, transportation was more greatly dreaded than hanging itself. He claims in his writing to have had three years' close contact with the prisoners in Newgate, often acting as their amanuensis, and that letters, sometimes four or five a day, were regularly received at the prison containing descriptions or drawings of prisoners' punishments. The advice on almost every occasion was 'Go slap up, and be hanged at once, rather than come here'; in other words, play for high stakes, get yourself hanged or acquitted. Repeatedly it was the same prisoners who, having served their sentence, were caught and imprisoned again. One of the principal causes for this was the great unnevenness of sentencing. This is hardly surprising when he points out that the average length of a trial was eight-and-a-half minutes and that between fifty and sixty persons were each held in readiness in the dock under the court.

The hard core of criminals were extremely calculating and felt that statistics were in their favour; first—of not being caught; second—if caught, of being acquitted; third—of getting away with a small sentence.

Death, in the abstract, was no deterrent but transportation was. Transportation might have been a deterrent but it was wrongly used. It was the uncertainty of how it was applied that robbed it of its sting. One day it would be passed on a prisoner for stealing a penny tart, while the very next day old and experienced pickpockets would get off with prison sentences of one or two months. Hardened felons calculated that only one in four of those convicted would be transported and it was a common belief among them that the judges were afraid to transport more than a certain number because of fears of clogging the system. There was some justification, in fact, for their belief that sentencing was a matter of chance—'that in the same day, and for a like crime, one man will be sentenced to transportation for life, while another may be let off for a month's imprisonment, and yet both equally bad characters'. At least three-quarters of the prisoners at every sessions were old hands. Short sentences they did not mind, considering four months' freedom out of every twelve a fair return.

'Go along, time!' they cry; only three months and a teazing. Never mind! that's over in ten minutes; (meaning the flogging); I would take one for each month, if the old fellow (the judge) would let me off the imprisonment.'

Out of 2500 convicted each year, about one-quarter were released and of the remainder (something under 2,000), about 800 were transported. It was possible for the hardened criminal to escape several sentences before being transported. One man was sentenced seventeen times before this happened.

The transports were taken out of Newgate in drafts of twenty-five. They shuffled through the streets, Newgate fashion, two-by-two, in their irons, at dawn, some drunk, some swearing and others abusing the spectators, to the lighters at Blackfriars where they would be taken down-river for embarkation. Some of them would have only been given three or four hours notice of when and where they were being taken. This was done after they had been locked up for the night and only then would the turnkeys call out the names of those who were sailing the next day. Part of this was deliberately done to shorten the leave-takings and to forestall demonstrations outside the prison gate by family and friends. Another reason for such short notice was that after the names had been called out there was generally a riot of some sort, with prisoners wrecking as much of the prison interiors as they could. Just as much damage seems to have been done, however, by the prisoners who were staying as by those who were leaving and who took the blame.

Women who were to be transported were similarly ironed, only in their case a chain was fastened to iron hoops about their waist, leg or ankle and, sometimes, all three. In transit this chain would be linked to a line of women so that one could not move without dragging the others with her. Not unnaturally such treatment added greatly to their brutalization.

Although transportation was widely regarded as a worse sentence than death the unnevenness of sentencing made it ineffective as a deterrent and, together with the chances of an acquittal, offered no real deterrent to crime. One glaring example of its unfairness was the case of two butchers, one old, the other young, who were found guilty of stealing a breast of mutton from their master. Although the older man had witnesses to testify to his former good character, and the other none, the older man was sentenced to fourteen years transportation and the younger six months imprisonment in the House of Correction! The prosecuting counsel took the unusual step of petitioning the Secretary of State on the man's behalf and confirmed that he himself had given the man a good character. These sort of cases simply reinforced a nineteenth-century aphorism among thieves that 'the biggest rogues get off the best'.

> The scene in the several yards of Newgate on the sentence-days, after the judgements have been passed, defies any description on paper. Some will be seen skipping and jumping about for hours, frenzied with joy at the very unexpectedly mild sentence passed on them; others are cursing, and swearing, calling down imprecations on the Recorder, for having, as they say, so unfairly measured out justice; all agreeing there is no proportion in the punishments to the crimes.

Black Dog of Newgate

> But if I could raise a small Sum—Would not twenty Guineas, think you, move him?—Of all the Arguments in the way of Business, the Perquisite is the most prevailing.—Your Father's Perquisites for the Escape of Prisoners must amount to a considerable Sum in the Year. Money well tim'd, and properly apply'd, will do anything.

> *John Gay, The Beggar's Opera*

In law there was no legal obligation to feed prisoners except felons who were awaiting execution. The Vagabonds Act (1572) empowered but did not compel magistrates to levy rates for providing for prisoners. Since this is almost 400 years after the prison came into being it adds point to the treatment of earlier prisoners and instances such as the gaol delivery of 1341 which was ordered by Edward III because so many prisoners were 'dying of hunger and oppression'.

Some such incident is the genesis of the famous 'Black Dog of Newgate' of which there are several explanations. By some it was thought to be a black stone in the condemned cell on which a prisoner had dashed out his brains; by another it was thought to be the black conscience of some of the

The Black Dog of Newgate. The title page of Luke Hutton's pamphlet circa 1596.

prisoners; by far the most vivid explanation is that it was an act of cannibalism in the reign of Henry II, at the beginnings of the prison, when starving prisoners were forced to eat other inmates to survive; according to the story, one was a poor scholar whom they judged 'passing good meate' but he returned to haunt them in the shape of a black dog 'ready with his ravening Jawes to teare out their Bowels . . . whereupon such a nightly feare grew amongst them, that it turned to a Frenzie, and from a Frenzie to desperation, in which Desperation they killed the Keeper; and so many of them escaped forth, but yet whithersoever they came or went, they imagined the blacke Dog to follow . . .'. Others thought the black dog only appeared the night before an execution when its ghostly form was seen to glide through the streets before the prison. By the sixteenth century it was used in an entirely different context; the authority is Luke Hutton's *The Black Dog of Newgate*, published about 1569. Hutton himself was hanged for highway robbery but his pamphlet was written while he was in Newgate or possibly soon after his release. The 'black dog', as Hutton uses it, was one 'who, in the Name of Service and Office, were, as it were, Servants of Newgate', and was no better than a villain masquerading as gaoler, turnkey or coney-catcher, which was an early name for the thief-takers. This duality is what he describes in his image of the Black Dog:

> Then did I fix mine eye upon this beast
> Who did appear first in the shape of man,
>
>   ★   ★   ★
>
> But in a trice he did transform his shape,
> Which broke a treble horror to my heart.
> A Cerebus, nay, worse, he thrice at wide did gape,
> His ears all snakes, curling, they will not part;
> Coal-black his hue, like torches glow his eyes,
> His breath does poison, smoke from his nostrils flies.
>
> His countenance ghastly, fearful, grim, and pale.
> His foamy mouth still gapeth for his prey;
> With tiger's teeth he spares none to assail,
> His lips hell-gates, o'erpainted with decay,
> His tongue the clapper, sounding woeful knell,
> Tolling poor men to ring a peal in hell.

By the early eighteenth century the 'black dog' connotations still lingered on though in a very muted form. There was a phrase 'Making the Black Dog Walk', which was a way of describing the prisoners' brutal treatments of new inmates who refused to pay 'garnish' and were punished by having their bedding, money and clothing forcibly taken and they themselves thrown into some stinking cess-pit. 'Garnish' was a phrase that the debtors used but which seems to have crept into use by all the prisoners gradually; it was in common usage by the late sixteenth century and in its legal sense, as defined in the dictionary, is: 'To serve notice on (a person) for the purpose of attaching money belonging to a debtor.' Debtors were supposed to be provided weekly with bread and water by their creditors (it was over 200 years before water was piped into the gaol and then it was an act of private charity), and it is not too difficult to see how such a definition could be wrenched slightly out of context to apply to the prisoners generally. 'Garnish' was demanded not only by the prisoners but by the turnkeys and others and was regarded as part of their lawful perquisites. As it was not until the eighteenth century that the latter began to be paid wages by the keeper, it is clear that many prisoners would have lost nearly everything of value before they had been many hours in the gaol.

Incredibly, 'garnish' continued to be paid well into the nineteenth century. At that time, those who could pay the admittance fee of three shillings gained entry into either the master's side or the cabin side; garnish was 13*s*. 4*d*. and a gallon of beer for the master's side, and a guinea entry for the cabin side with a gallon of beer on release; for the common side it was a few shillings less. Those who could not pay 'garnish' were tyrannized in a number of ways. Buxton wrote.

> The prisoner, after his commitment is made out, is handcuffed to a file of perhaps a dozen wretched persons in a similar situation and marched through the streets, sometimes a considerable distance, followed by a crowd of impudent and insulting boys, exposed to the gaze and to the stare of every passenger. The moment he enters prison, irons are hammered on him; then he is cast into the midst of a compound of all that is disgusting and depraved. At night, he is locked up in a narrow cell, with perhaps half-a-dozen of the worst thieves in London, or as many vagrants, whose rags are alive and in actual motion with vermin. He may find himself in bed and in bodily contact between a robber and a murderer or between a man with a foul disease on one side and one with an infectious disorder on the other.

He quotes the lawyer who was sent to Newgate in a coach, handcuffed to a highwayman who was already marked for the gallows. For the next two weeks he slept in the same bed with the highwayman on one side and a murderer on the other. The other prisoners viewed him with considerable suspicion, because he was a lawyer, and although he drank with them to be sociable, they decreed that he was outside their prison laws. He was humiliated in numerous ways, and eventually broken by their petty persecutions. They had their own-style 'courts' and any charge would do to bring him to trial. He could be tried if he stood too near the fire, if he coughed, left a door open or touched something that didn't belong to him. The judge, usually the oldest thief, wore a ragged towel of knots on his head which had been tied so as to simulate the judge's wig; everyone had to call him 'My Lord'. Bribes of any sort could easily influence his decisions. The worst sentence that he could impose was that of the pillory; this was done by forcing the prisoner's head through the chair legs to which would be tied his outstretched arms. He would have to stay like this until he was released. The lawyer 'by insensible degrees [he] began to lose his repugnance to their society, caught their flash terms and sung their songs, was admitted to their revels, and acquired, in place of habits of perfect sobriety, a taste for spirits'. When his wife visited him she was subjected to all sorts of humiliations. One day she found him pale, very ill and dirty with the other prisoners gathered round and jeering at them both; he had been made deliberately drunk and, before she left, his wife was told that she must pay his share of five shillings or he would be stripped of his remaining clothes.

It was for such reasons as these that those who could pay the master's side entrance fee did so plus the extra 2s. 6d. that gave them the use of a barrack-style bedstead with a turning space of nineteen inches. This money was necessary to part-finance the running of the prison as without it, so the keeper declared, he could not pay the turnkeys' wages.

A brace of public guardians. By Thomas Rowlandson (1800).

By the adoption of a kind of Lancastrian system the prisoners themselves were constrained to play a part in prison management. Four keeper's partners, who existed by 1633 and had a room of their own by 1671, fixed irons upon their fellow-prisoners and exerted a crude discipline over them by striking them with the bull's pizzles with which they were armed; hence their alternative name, 'truncheon officers'. The partners, who had their own assistants called Swabbers, intended as cleaners, seem for their violence to have lost authority about 1730. The Debtors chose a steward or stewards to administer their charities. On the master debtors' side the stewards collected garnish, spent it on supplies for their wards, and were aided by constables. The turnkeys chose cellarmen for the master felons' side. The cellarman seems to have had some similar regulatory functions, though there were no charities to administer. They partly monopolized the sale of liquor. Such, at any rate, is an approximate picture of the economy in the earlier eighteenth century.

Howard's inquiry

The general prevalence and spread of wickedness in prisons, and abroad by the discharged prisoners, will now be as easily accounted for, as the propagation of disease. It is often said, 'A prison pays no debts', I am sure it may be added, that a prison needs no morals. Sir John Fielding, in his Plan for preventing Robberies, observes, that 'a criminal discharged—generally by the next sessions, after the execution of his comrades, becomes the captain of a gang of his own raising',—improved, no doubt, in skill by the company he kept in gaol. And petty offenders who are committed to Bridewell for a year or two, and spend that time, not in hard labour, but in idleness and wicked company, or are sent for that time to county gaols, generally grow desperate, and come out fitted for the perpetration of any villainy. I scruple not to affirm, that half the robberies committed in and about London, are planned in the prisons by that dreadful assemblage of criminals and the number of idle people who visit them.

John Howard, The State of the Prisons in England and Wales (1780)

Howard's inquiry into the state of the prisons began when he was Sheriff of Bedford in 1773. What started as a local investigation turned into a national and finally an international look at prisons and prison life. He wrote that he was frequently asked what precautions he took against gaol-fever. He replied that his faith, temperance and cleanliness were his preservatives and that he never entered a prison or hospital before breakfast and in an offensive room seldom drew a deep breath! He explained that readers could judge of the malignity of the poisonous atmospheres he had to penetrate 'when I assure him, that my clothes were in my first journeys so offensive, that in a post-chaise I could not bear the windows drawn up; and was therefore often obliged to travel on horse-back. The leaves of my memorandum book were often so tainted, that I could not use it till after spreading it an hour or two before the fire: and even my antidote, a vial of vinegar, has, after using it in a few prisons, become intolerably disagreeble. I did not wonder that in those journeys many gaolers made excuses; and did not go with me into the felons wards.'

Howard's first visit to Newgate, published in 1777, was while Dance was completing his building. Howard did not think it a model to be followed and thought it had some 'manifest errors' which it was too late now to point out; he added ominously: 'All I will say, is, that without more than ordinary care, the prisoners in it will be in great danger of the gaol-fever.' Dance had retained fifteen cells from the old building, where the condemned prisoners were kept, and was planning to annexe these to the new building. There were five on each floor, the smallest cells on the ground floor being nine feet by six; each cell had a double grated window, doors four inches thick, the

John Howard, prison reformer. By M. Brown.

walls lined with planks held in place by broad-headed nails, and furnished with a barrack-style bedstead. Howard was told 'that criminals who had affected an air of boldness during their trial, and appeared quite unconcerned at the pronouncing sentence upon them, were struck with horror, and shed tears, when brought to these darksome solitary abodes'.

Howard went twice to the chapel which he thought 'plain and neat'. Below the visitors' gallery were pews for the male felons; on either side were galleries, one for women and the other for debtors. The few prisoners that were there were attentive but the service was constantly interrupted by outside noises which the Ordinary assured him was always the case. Clearly the religious service was not compulsory, as Howard continued that since the prisoners would not go to chapel they should be locked up during the service.

At his next visit he found the prison clean and 'free from offensive scents'.

Among his statistics (August 1779) Howard noted that there were 51 debtors and 141 felons; from the latter figure: 91 convicts and fines had a penny loaf a day. That same year the keeper, Richard Akerman, was asked how convicted prisoners could live on such an amount. His answer was that they did not and that most of them were supplied with money and provisions by their friends. For those who did not have anyone to provide for them he provided, at his own expense, a broth made of coarse pieces of meat. Debtors had eight stones of beef delivered every Saturday from the chamber of London; fines had four stones; and some years the felons had eight stones. In addition the debtors benefited by several legacies amounting to £52 5s. 8d. a year. Other donations included sixty-four stone of beef and five dozen of bread, though whether of stone or loaves Howard doesn't clarify.

From the seventeenth century, and probably before, the money levied by magistrates was used to buy bread—which was delivered each Monday. Each penny loaf weighed 8 oz, but Howard's own experience was that the weight could fluctuate with the price of bread; generally it did stay somewhere near the 8oz mark but nearer double the weight could have been purchased when the allowance was first fixed. Elsewhere he said that it was normal for the loaf to be eaten in some circumstances at breakfast which meant that the prisoner would often have to starve until his next allowance. Prisoners often came out so starved that they could not walk or were incapable of labour. On subsequent visits Howard found in 1782 that the penny loaf weighed 8½ oz and, after the prisoners had petitioned for an increase, in 1783 that there was a 1½d. loaf weighing 13 oz. The felons on the common side had the 1½d. loaf. The past history of the prison showed that there had been regular complaints about short weight; at one time bread was weighed in the gaol but the scales disappeared and were not replaced until many years afterwards in 1737.

Howard revisited the gaol after it had been rebuilt following the Gordon Riots destruction. It was rebuilt to the same plan. The men's quadrangle was divided into three courts: in the first were those who paid 3s. 6d. for a bed, in the next were the poorer felons, and in the third were the women. Below the chapel were cells for refractory prisoners. Two rooms adjoining the condemned cells had been built for an infirmary; in one of the rooms there were sixteen sick. The surgeon's salary to treat all prisoners was £100 per annum; he thought that the prison should have its own physician and apothecary who might effectively minimize the risk of infection and silence the county gaolers whom he had often heard complain: 'The distemper was brought from Newgate by prisoners removed from thence by habeas corpus.' In the past century there had been temporary alliances with St Bartholomew's hospital with physicians visiting the prison to relieve the prisoners' suffering, but such efforts seem to have been short-lived because

N E W G A T E.

GAOLER, *Richard Akerman.*

Salary,	£200.		
Fees,	Debtors,	-	£0 : 8 : 10.
	Felons,	-	0 : 18 : 10.
	Mifdemeanours or Fines,	0 : 14 : 10.
	Tranfports,	-	0 : 14 : 10.
Licence,	Beer and Wine.		

PRISONERS,

Allowance, Debtors, ⎫ a penny loaf a day. *(See Remarks.)*
     Felons, ⎭

Garnifh, Debtors, £0 : 5 : 6.
    Felons &c. 0 : 2 : 6.

Number,   Debtors. Felons &c.   Debtors. Felons &c.

1775, March 5,	33,	190.	1776, Dec. 26,	33,	152.
1776, —— 1,	38,	129.	1779, Aug. 16,	51,	141.
—— May 17,	46,	212.			

CHAPLAIN, Rev. Mr. *Villette.*

Duty,   Sunday twice; every day prayers;
      once a month facrament.
Salary,   £35, &c. *(See Remarks.)*

SURGEON, Mr. *Olney.*

Salary,   £50, for all prifoners.

Table of salaries and fees (from Howard's The State of the Prisons in England and Wales*).*

they interrupted the hospital duties. Possibly the threat of gaol-fever was another deterrent and on one occasion, at least, when their help was sought, surgeons refused to attend to amputate a man's legs that had 'mortified'. As result the hospital provided an apothecary for nine months but withdrew its help because of a lack of clothing and bedding. The surgeon who had been called in to amputate, continued to act as prison surgeon in a private capacity as did his successor. At first they were compensated with freedoms but by 1777 were in receipt of a salary of £50 per annum. By 1784 this had doubled.

The keeper's official salary was £200 a-year; until a few years before he had a beer and wine licence which had been worth a further £200. Together, with his fees, his annual earnings had averaged out at about £800 a year. At

London fc. A TABLE of FEES to be taken by the Gaoler or Keeper of Newgate within the said City of London for any Prisoner or Prisoners committed or coming into Gaol or Chamber-Rent there or discharge from thence in any *Civil Action* settled and established the nineteenth day of December in the third year of the reign of his Majesty King George the Second *Annoque Domini* 1729 pursuant to an Act of Parliament lately made intituled An Act for the Relief of *Debtors* with respect to the Imprisonment of their Persons.

	£.	S.	D.
Every prisoner on the master-side shall pay to the keeper for his entrance fee	o	3	o
Every prisoner on the master-side shall pay for chamber-room use of bed bedding and sheets to the keeper there being two in a bed and no more each *per* week	o	1	3
Every prisoner on the said master-side who at his own desire shall have a bed to himself, shall pay to the keeper for chamber-room use of bed bedding and sheets *per* week	o	2	6
Every debtor shall pay to the keeper for his discharging fee	o	6	10
And to all the turnkeys two shillings and no more	o	2	o

No other fee for the use of chamber bed bedding or sheets or upon the commitments or discharge of any prisoner on any civil action

Edwd Becher	ROBT RAYMOND
Robt Alsop	R. EYRE
Ino Barnard	THOS PENGELLY

Mr. Akerman shewed me another table of fees, which was given him for his direction when he commenced keeper. It is as follows :

FEES to be taken by the Keeper of Newgate.

	£.	S.	D.
For every debtor's discharge	o	8	10
For every felon's discharge	o	18	10
For every misdemeanour	o	14	10
Every debtor's entrance on the master's side	o	3	o
Every felon's entrance on the master's side	o	10	6
Every person admitted into the press-yard	3	3	o
For every transport's discharge	o	14	10
For every bailable warrant	3	6	8

Table of fees (from Howard's The State of the Prisons in England and Wales).

his death he left an estate of £20,000. The income of six to ten turnkeys had been paid out of his income and the previous keeper's since 1732, which does suggest that there were other undeclared sources of income. For many years several taphouses and cellars had flourished in the gaol selling a wide variety of drinks, including beer, brandy and fine wines. These were leased by the keeper either to the turnkeys or the turnkeys' wives and flourished until 1751 when the sale of spirits in prisons was prohibited by Parliament. All prison taps were closed down by 1785. In addition there was a table of fees.

Akerman's and Howard's evidence on conditions, though given on different occasions and the latter's evidence not always specifically relating to Newgate, can be usefully offset as counterpoint to one another. In 1782, at the time of Howard's later visit, there were 291 prisoners—225 men and 66 women; 100 of these were transports, 89 were fines, 91 were under sentence of death and the remainder were awaiting trial. Some of the condemned had been a long time sick and were languishing in their cells.

Akerman said 'that he had often observed a dejection of spirits among the prisoners in Newgate, which had the effect of disease, and many had died broken-hearted and they were, usually, felons better behaved, and less abandoned than the others: that the prisoners were obliged to wash themselves, but it was very difficult to compel some of them . . . all the male prisoners accused of felonies, or misdemeanours, associated together in the day time; the debtors were separated from the felons night and day, and the males from the females; the convicts had no employment . . . when they were unruly, he locked them up, and put irons on their legs; they seem to dread solitary confinement.'

Howard's theory on such dejection of spirits, which he linked to gaol-fever and the lack of fresh air and cleanliness, was the sudden change of diet and lodging which so affected them that it was common to see stout robust young men sicken and die in a sort time with little apparent illness.

> These are ironed, and thrust into close offensive dungeons, some of them without straw or other bedding; in which they continue, in winter, sixteen or eighteen hours out of the twenty four, in utter inactivity and immersed in the noxious effluvia of their own bodies. . . . Their diet is at the same time low and scanty; they are generally without firing; and the powers of life soon become incapable of resisting so many causes of sickness and despair.

Howard's remarks on prisons in general were that he had found few prisons abroad as dirty and offensive as those he had found at home. In some cells the floors were not just damp but under an inch or two of water; instead of being given bedsteads prisoners had to float bedding, which might be straw, on the stone flags. Usually there was no bedding as its provision would have eaten into the gaoler's cost. When straw was provided it would not be changed for some months or at least until it had been worn to dust. Some prisoners were reduced to sleeping on rags or on the bare floors. In Newgate, Akcrman charged 2s. 6d. for a single bed on the master's side or half price if they would share it. Another reason Howard found for cells being so close was that gaolers would brick up windows rather than pay the hated window tax!

Garnish continued to be a common custom and not just peculiar to London where it was called in some gaols 'chummage'. Newcomers were told 'Pay or strip'. Those who did have money reluctantly surrendered it and those that did not had to hand over bedding or clothing to be converted into cash for an evening's hard drinking. Howard quotes the case of four men who were indicted at the Old Bailey in 1730 for robbing a prisoner of two half guineas, two sixpences and two half-pence under pretext of taking garnish. Not only were they found guilty of assault and robbery but plainly as a deterrent—but ineffective—sentenced to death.

Money that was not spent on drink went on gaming. Entertainments in Newgate and other prisons included such pastimes as cards, dice, skittles, billiards, fives, tennis and other games.

Howard's condemnation was reserved for such practices as putting such heavy irons on prisoners that it was painful for them to move about or sleep. (Macheath in John Gay's *The Beggar's Opera* was offered a choice of fetters ranging in size from one to ten; the heaviest were the most expensive.) Some prisoners wore their irons even in court but in London there was a special block which could free them in a minute or two (it should be remembered that some of the irons, particularly handcuffs, were riveted on). Howard was especially condemnatory of the practice, which had probably originated in torture, when the prisoners were brought up to receive their sentence and the judge asked: 'What have you to say why judgement of death and execution should not be awarded against you?' The executioner would then slip a whipcord noose about their thumbs. The origins of this were obscure, unless as a means of compelling prisoners to answer, and ought to have long been abolished.

Some of his suggested improvements were to help the many prisoners who had been denied their tools of trade for fear that they would use them to escape. The exercise of such skills was normally allowed by the prison regime and was the only way that prisoners could buy extra food and necessities. Their plight was aggravated by the fact that many of them had their families with them, despite the appalling risks of disease. Without their tools they could not live and Howard had often seen them eating a miserable water soup, which was nothing more than bread boiled in water, while bitterly complaining that they were being starved to death. When they asked the magistrates for food the official reply was very often:'Let them work or starve', which was virtually a death sentence to them.

Some of Howard's suggestions seem so commonsense that it is astonishing they should have to have been made at all. They are: that prisoners' rooms should be regularly swept and washed down; that new inmates should be washed and made to wear a uniform, and their clothes disinfected; that there should be a prison alarm bell; that straw beds should be encased in canvas and laid not on the floor but on beds; that there should be proper washing facilities; that no prisoner should have to pay fees or garnish; that the taps should be abolished (certainly that no gaoler should have a financial stake in them); bread should be supplied by weight and not by price; finally, that inspectors should be appointed to visit the gaols to see what was happening inside them.

Here at least the City had pursued an erratic course which began in medieval times when inspectors were appointed to visit the gaol after a revolt in 1456—when the prisoners 'brak theyr pryson and went upon the ledys and fawgth agayn the Cytyzins and kept the Gate a grete while but at last they were ovircomyn and after sore ponysshid with Iryns and ffetyrs'. The inspectors (two curates and two commoners) were there to hear complaints, to make sure that alms were being fairly distributed, to check the water supply and similar matters. Some inspections were carried out, such as in 1488 when they directed that the keeper was to charge no more than 1d. for a penny loaf or 2d. for a gallon of beer. Failure to comply meant a 20s. fine for the first offence, 40s. for the second, and suspension from office for five years for a third occurrence.

Gradually such visits subsided until in 1521 there was a complaint that the appointment of inspectors had not been made for a great while. No more seem to have been made until 1681 when two aldermen and four common councillors were regularly appointed to inspect the prisons. This continued, with declining interest, into the next century 'and therefore more than forty years before Howard's first journey, they pursued a course of steady if lethargic reformation'.

Such inspections reinforced Howard's contention that prisons were not gaolers' private property to do with as they liked. Elsewhere he had often asked gaolers whether the sheriffs, justices or town magistrates visited their gaols. The answer was usually 'Not at all'; or 'Those gentlemen think that if they came into my gaol, they should soon be in their graves'; or 'The justices think the inside of my house too close for them; they satisfy themselves with viewing the outside.' As Howard said, if this indifference continued, then a thorough reformation of the prisons became impossible and any improvements that had been made would soon be lost and a reversion to the old conditions would be inevitable.

That the inspections had become more desultory and the neglect by the prison staff just as gross was borne out by Howard's final visit, published the year before his death in 1790, which said that on that visit he found nearly 151 women crowded into three or four rooms, the old as well as the young, some of whom had been confined there for more than two years. A similar state existed on the men's side where there were many boys of twelve to fourteen years old, some of them almost naked. In the men's infirmary there were only seven beds and, at his last visit because there were twenty sick, some of them naked and covered with sores, they were forced to lie on the floor on a rug. There were four sick in the women's infirmary, which had only one window and no beds. The sewers stank and the prison was dirty. The keeper no longer maintained a tap. His salary had been increased by £50 to compensate him. Instead, some of the debtors had beer for sale and on the felons' side one prisoner was selling cans of beer!

Parliamentary inquiries 1814 and 1818

. . . .but the want of sufficient room to classify the prisoners—the entire absence, as far as the men and boys are concerned, of all employment—the promiscuous assemblage of persons of all descriptions, ages, and characters of crime, have deeply impressed your committee with the opinion, that no one can enter the walls of Newgate without going from thence more depraved and corrupted than when first committed thereto.

Report on Prisons in the City of London and Borough of Southwark (1818)

Howard's pioneering work was the basis for the penological reforms that continued throughout the nineteenth century, but in its criticisms of Newgate it can scarcely be considered more than anecdotal and a detailed analysis of conditions inside the gaol does not appear until the penitentiary reports of 1811, 1814 and 1818. The theme of all three reports was one of classification or, in the phrasing of the 1818 Committee: 'The whole system of enlightened jurisprudence is devised for the prevention of crime not of abstract punishment.' Classification was a way of separating the tried from the untried, the first offender from the irreclaimable and the beginning of a structure which could be imposed on the whole system.

On one thing the reports were all agreed and that was that Newgate was wholly inadequate in every way for the purpose for which it was intended. However, after publication of the 1811 report, a start was made the following year on a tentative classification of prisoners. The Chapel Yard, which was set aside for the experiment, could hold up to seventy prisoners. Classification was by whether a prisoner was (a) charged with a felony or had been convicted or (b)whether he had been charged with a misdemeanour only. With such a broad classification this was bound to cause some unfairness as some of the offences, though technically felonies, were far less serious than some of the misdemeanours. Prisoners' feelings that the system was unjust were aggravated by the fact that all those in the first category were ironed, except prisoners with good behaviour records, and those in the second category were not. The average weight of the irons was 3 to 4 lbs, which could be doubled if the prisoner was troublesome.

By day the two sides could mingle in the exercise yard but at night they slept in wards about fifteen-foot long on inclined wood ramps, separated by a gangway, with a beam at one end which doubled as their pillow; instead of beds they had rugs of hemp. This arrangement gave them a sleeping space of about nineteen inches each, but this could be less if the prison numbers increased, which they did at this time—far in excess of the safety margin of 500 prisoners—to more than 800. Part of this problem was caused by the slowness in removing transports, who could be delayed on occasions from six months to a year. At one committee visit 150 prisoners were awaiting removal. The wards could normally hold 30 to 40 prisoners but at times reached up to between 50 and 60. The same overcrowding occurred in the fifteen condemned cells where there were sometimes 60 to 70 prisoners under sentence of death sharing three to four to a cell.

The 1814 Committee was particularly censorious of three long-standing abuses which were: the keeper's fees and the way in which the prison was funded; garnish; and the continuance of debtors in a criminal gaol. Dealing with the question of fees the committee was scathing: 'No part of a Gaoler's income ought to be exacted from his Prisoners. Such an income, frequently ill paid, to a humane Gaoler, leaves him also too much open to the imputation of harshness, whilst it gives to a harsh Gaoler a power of oppression; it also leads to the employment of too small a number, and a inferior description of servants.' The committee questioned the keeper, John Newman, who had been in office for about ten years. When asked how much his fees averaged he refused to answer but volunteered the information that his salary and fees combined paid for the running costs of the prison; he explained that about a third of this was covered by his salary of £450 a year and the balance by his fees and rents which left him a profit of between £600 and £1000.

The prison was organized into three parts; there was the Debtors' side which consisted of three buildings—the master's side, the cabin side and the common side with a room set to one side where they could work at their trades; there was the criminal side, which consisted of six yards—including the Chapel Yard and the Press Yard— where the condemned prisoners were held; and lastly the woman's side, which was built for seventy prisoners although here, as elsewhere, numbers could fluctuate. The ideal number was fewer than 500 prisoners; when the committee made its report there were 110 debtors and 317 criminal prisoners although only a few months previously, in January, the numbers had risen to 822.

Newman did not interfere, or tried not to, with the way that the prisoners organized their lives. His neglect was almost as great as the Ordinary's the Rev Brownlow Ford, who had been prison chaplain for sixteen years. From his own account of his duties he seems to have performed the minimum required of him; he gave the sacrament only to those under sentence of death, saw only those who came to chapel and didn't consider it worth instructing or giving comfort to the boys that came into the prison, some of them 10 years-old and younger. These boys were ironed if they were charged with felonies, because they were in the prison for such a short time.

Newman's toleration extended to garnish, which was levied on everyone throughout the prison. Those on the master's side didn't benefit from the charity donations of meat, coal, etc., because they were paying for a better form of accommodation; this was 13s. 6d. admission 2s. 6d. a-week for a bed; there was a further sub-division of the master's side which was called the state side, where the admission fee was 2 guineas and the prisoners paid 10s. 6d. a week for a bed or 7s. if they shared. Newman stressed that he didn't interfere with the way that they ran the master's side, but one presumes that the garnish that was levied was spent, as in other parts of the prison, on coals, candles, salt, pepper, wine and beer—the latter sold at the same price as at public houses outside as theoretically nobody was supposed to make a profit.

Charity coal and meat was given to the debtors in the cabin and common sides. Prisoners who refused to pay garnish were 'chalked' from the fire, which meant that they might not get a share of the charity meat or, if they did, that they would not be allowed to cook it or forced to eat it raw or possibly sell it for something that could be eaten uncooked. The debtors here, as on the master's side, were expected to buy their own brooms, mops and buckets and clean their wards themselves.

On the criminal side such items were provided, as the prisoners were serving sentences, and the food allowance was slightly better than the debtors; but, so the committee reported, it was 'not sufficient properly to support life, without the assistance of friends, and casual charity . . .'.

In its summing up, the only bright spot in the committee's findings was that a prison for debtors was being built on the north side of the City, in Whitecross Street, and when completed would greatly ease the overcrowding that Newgate was subjected to. As for the prison generally the committee concluded that most of its evils and inadequacies proceeded from its being wholly inadequate for its purpose.

Elizabeth Fry

The year before, in the winter of 1813, a friend urged Elizabeth Fry to visit the poor women in Newgate. At this time she was 33 years old, the mother of eight children, the daughter of a Quaker merchant-banker. The friend had been dismayed by what he had seen in the women's wards; even the

Elizabeth Fry, prison reformer. Painting after C.R. Leslie.

keeper, Newman, was reluctant to visit these wards which had long been known as 'Hell above ground'. He had tried to frighten off his visitor by telling him that at the very least he was likely to have his clothes torn off. Nearly three hundred women were crowded into the two wards—this was four times the official figure. Some were sick, others sleeping on straw which had worn away, some in hammocks and several newborn babies, naked and crying. In this cramped space they cooked, ate, slept, drank and fought and gave birth. The only persons responsible for them were two turnkeys, father and son. With a number of friends Mrs Fry made up a bundle of baby clothes and went to the prison. Newman was reluctant to let her enter and at best could only persuade her to take off her watch to stop it from being stolen. Once inside Mrs Fry and a friend clothed the babies and offered such comfort as they could to the mothers. She was greatly moved by the sight of two prisoners stripping a dead baby to clothe one that was living.

She returned again the next day but had to force herself to go inside. She later tried to describe the experience but could not.

> All I tell thee is a faint picture of the reality; the filth, the closeness of the rooms, the ferocious manners and expressions of the women towards each other, and the abandoned wickedness, which everything bespoke, are quite indescribable.

She made one last visit that winter and then no more for another three years. In that time she gave birth to two more children and mourned the death of another. Eventually it was her compassion and an overwhelming desire to help the children that brought her back to the gaol.

She renewed her visits at Christmas 1816. Since her last visit the women had been given more space to move about and now occupied some extra wards and cells. This seems to have been the only improvement. 'Hell above ground' still justified its name. Mrs Fry found that conditions were much the same. She and the other helpers that went with her were 'witnesses of the dreadful proceedings that went forward on the female side of the prison; the begging, swearing, gaming, fighting, singing, dancing, dressing up in men's clothes; the scenes are too bad to be described, so that we did not think it suitable to admit young persons with us'. Through the bars that separated them from visitors the women would thrust spoons tied to the end of sticks and shriek for alms which they would fight over, spend on drink or gamble on cards. Running among them were about thirty children, many of them almost naked, pining for food, fresh air and exercise.

Instead of preaching at them or treating them like animals, which is how they were normally handled, Mrs Fry asked the prisoners, many of them thieves or prostitutes, whether there was nothing they could do to help the children. When she suggested a school the idea was greeted with tears of joy, almost abandon, by these desperate women. Her most difficult task was to convince the authorities that such an idea was practicable. At a meeting with the two sheriffs, the Ordinary and the keeper, she persisted in her attempts to get their agreement despite their polite acknowledgment that the idea was a good one but the women would turn such a school into a roughhouse. The first meeting came to nothing and at a second she forced them to admit that the only real objection they had was that there was nowhere suitable for a classroom. Triumphantly Mrs Fry went back to the prisoners, who agreed to give up part of their accommodation and let her use one of the cells. At this the authorities agreed to let her try her 'benevolent, but almost hopeless experiment'. The prisoners chose from among themselves a young educated woman, who had been committed for

Mrs Fry's door circa *1900.*

stealing a watch, to give the first lesson to the school, most of whose pupils were under seven years old. Older children and adults also wanted to benefit, and one of Mrs Fry's helpers said much later that entering the school was like stepping into a den of importuning wild beasts, with half-naked women struggling and shrieking to be heard, and recalled the shudder that went through her as the door clanged behind. For those who had been excluded there was only despair and a feeling that such exclusion was an extension of their punishment.

Gradually Mrs Fry and her helpers, through their daily visits, the gifts of clothing, food and Bibles, began to make changes. Seeing how bad conditions were, Mrs Fry formed a committee, consisting of a clergyman's wife and eleven members of the Society of Friends, which voluntarily undertook to work daily in the prison for the benefit of the women prisoners. Although she was apt to treat the women as erring servants Mrs Fry, far ahead of her time, always consulted them and got their total agreement to any changes proposed.

Her next step was to get them employment. Again there was the official opposition to her plans but she won over the keeper and sheriffs to her ideas, despite their feelings that the women would only steal the materials. The sheriffs' frankly expressed opinion was 'that it was in vain to expect such untamed and turbulent spirits would submit to the regulations of a woman armed with no legal authority, and unable to inflict any punishment'. Clearly much depended on the attitude of the prisoners themselves, but they agreed to be bound by a set of rules which was publicly discussed and voted on before the scheme began. The rules allowed for a matron to be appointed (this was an outside appointment with her wages being originally paid by the committee and subsequently by the Corporation of London). A yard-keeper and monitors were to be chosen from the women, who were to be divided into classes of twelve. There was to be no begging, gaming, swearing, card-playing, immoral conversation, novels, plays, improper books, any default of which was to be reported to the matron. The women were to be engaged in knitting, sewing or other suitable employment.

To find work for the women was more difficult. One of the committee approached the contractors who manufactured clothing for the convict settlement in Botany Bay. The firm guaranteed to buy all the prisoners' work, and when Mrs Fry gave her evidence to the 1818 committee she was able to tell them that the women had made in their first ten months about 20,000 articles of clothing which had earned them each 1s. 6d. a week. Some of this hard-earned money was voluntarily surrendered by the prisoners themselves to the female transports being sent to Botany Bay, where they were received more like prostitutes than servants. To make the partings easier, and to stop the drunkenness and destruction among the transports the night before they left the gaol, Mrs Fry persuaded Newman to let them travel in privacy in hackney coaches with the turnkeys, with herself in attendance, and avoid the humiliation, which is what they feared, of riding in chains in open carts as a public spectacle.

Mrs Fry was anxious to keep her experiment under wraps but the results were so successful that in one short month it was clear that it was succeeding. After a visit of inspection by the Lord Mayor and other influential officials the new rules were incorporated in the governing regulations. The change had been a dramatic one. A visitor wrote:

> The courtyard into which I was admitted, instead of being peopled with beings scarcely human, blaspheming, fighting, tearing each other's hair, or gaming with a filthy pack of cards for the very clothes they wore, which often did not suffice even for decency, presented a scene where stillness and propriety reigned. I was conducted by a decently-dressed person, the newly appointed yards-woman, to the door of a ward where, at the head of a long table sat a lady belonging to the Society of Friends. She was reading aloud to about sixteen women prisoners who were engaged in needlework around it. Each wore a clean looking blue apron and bib, with a ticket having a number on it suspended from her neck by a red tape. They all rose on my entrance, curtsied respectfully and then at a signal resumed their seats and employments. Instead of a scowl, leer, or ill-suppressed laugh, I observed upon their countenances an air of self-respect and gravity, a sort of consciousness of their improved character, and the altered position in which they were placed.

1818 inquiry

The 1818 Committee which was asked to 'Report on Prisons in the City of London and Borough of Southwark' drew attention to the fact that to survive at all prisoners had to have help from the outside. When Mrs Fry was asked by the committee what proportion of women would be in want without their assistance she replied that they normally dealt with eighty tried women and of these about ten lived well (some had poultry sent in), twenty very badly and the others were supported by friends. Four women and the same number of children had died in the previous ten months; all of them had been without the assistance of friends and capable of very little work. Some women were near naked when they came into the prison and had to be provided with clothes as did, at times, their babies.

The prison did not even provide basics such as towels, soap or basins. Some of these necessities, such as soap, had been bought from a £40 grant from the sheriffs' fund, but this grant was liable to fluctuate depending on the good will of the incumbents. Prisoners generally could bring in their own beds, if they possessed them, but the normal bed for most was a hemp mat worked with tar, to keep out the damp, and two rugs to sleep on or to cover themselves with. The turning space for each was 18 to 24 inches, but

A public whipping in the Sessions House Yard (from Jackson's New and Complete Newgate Calendar *1818).*

this could vary depending on the number of prisoners. Mrs Fry made the point that no matter how hard the women tried to keep themselves clean it was inevitable that they should be dirty again within the hour when thirty of them, and their children, were cooking, sleeping and washing in the one room.

The prison allowed only water to drink but porter could be sent in. Three years previously the women drank gin, and it was still possible to get drunk on beer. The daily allowance of food was 1 lb of brown bread which was cooked at the Giltspur Street Compter; the prisoners preferred white bread which, though it weighed 2 oz less, was not so coarse and sour and did not give them diarrhoea. They were given also 1 lb of meat twice a week (Mrs Fry described it as 'mouse-buttock, a nice, nourishing part'.), which was still insufficient to keep the prisoners healthy. There was still not enough food despite a new allowance which gave the prisoners a pint of gruel for breakfast and despite new cooking arrangements, this meant that their meat ration was halved (6½ oz when cooked) and spread over four days, alternating with meat one day and a quart of soup in which the meat had been cooked the previous day on the next; to this were added vegetables. Mrs Fry recommended lots of potatoes.

Another witness the committee heard was the Ordinary, the Rev Cotton. In the first flush of enthusiasm after his appointment in 1814 he had started a school for boys on the men's side. The numbers over the past four years had averaged between twenty and fifty but he had been quickly disillusioned by their attitude and indignantly felt that he had been cheated and plundered. Possibly in that first flush of enthusiasm he had financed the scheme himself, which from his angry attitude seems probable. His aim was to teach the boys shoemaking. Leather was bought and a shoemaker found to teach them; but the scheme was discontinued when it was discovered that the good leather had been sent out and replaced by bad, and that the boys, in a spirit of mischief, had then cut through the shoes after they had been paid for making them.

From then on his indifference seems to have grown as did his unspoken hostility (at least until some years later) to the success of Mrs Fry. The schoolmaster was a convict who had been convicted of slave-trading (not directly that is but he loaned his ship to a black king who had wanted it for slaving.) As the committee rightly pointed out, even if sincere, the teacher could not have the influence of a person of unblemished reputation! The boys had four hours of schooling each day, one or two hours of exercise when the men were locked up, and ten hours of idleness, the reverend explained. That was all, except for those who had been classified as felons: at the last sessions five of them were thirteen years old or younger; one of them was little more than nine years old. Despite their youth, because they had been charged with felony, they had to wear irons and be kept in the Press Yard.

The weariness and indifference of the Rev Cotton seeps through his evidence and never more so than when he is describing the condition of one of the boys who had been brought in who had no shoes, stockings, breeches, or waistcoat; he had borrowed a shirt from one of the other boys and wore a tattered greatcoat pinned in such a way as to hide his nakedness. The keeper had said there were no more clothes to hand out, and the Ordinary felt that he had done all that was required of his office when he pointed this boy out to the sheriffs as being in want. Nothing more was done for the boy and he stayed in that condition. Even more chilling was the attitude to those boys under sentence of death, not one of whom was admitted to the school.

The year before the committee made its report there had been a change of keeper; instead of Newman it was now William Brown. The changeover had been marked by the abolition of fees, which had been replaced by a salary of £500, free of taxes, and a house. When questioned, the keeper told the committee that he had abolished the long-standing abuse of garnish and that it was now very firmly a thing of the past. There had been a slight relaxation in the regulations relating to the use of irons; untried prisoners were now exempt but that was the only concession.

More space had been created by the completion of the Whitecross Street prison. Debtors had been moved out of Newgate which was now a criminal prison only. The committee in its conclusions thought that 'on the whole, as far as instruction permitted, the treatment of prisoners generally met with their approbation'. The prison fare did not appear worse or more severe than was consistent with such an establishment or injurious to the health of the prisoners. In this the committee was flying in the face of all the evidence that had been given to it. Members were disturbed that there was no proper classification of prisoners and no employment of any sort for the men. In this, the committee added, no blame was to be attached to the keeper. The true blame lay with the prison itself, which should have been more commodious and better constructed, but it was too much to expect of the City that it should be pulled down and a new one built to replace it.

The only recommendation that the committee felt that it could make was that Newgate should cease to be a custodial prison and be used exclusively instead for prisoners awaiting trial at the Sessions House.

Despite these advances to a reform of the system the law remained as severe as it had ever been. The 1818 Committee, though it found in those 'receptacles of wretchedness and crime, scenes so painful and repulsive to the feelings', found it necessary to recollect that certain hardships were 'necessary and unavoidable'. A decade or so after it made these remarks a young boy was committed to Newgate for possessing a watch which he had swapped with another boy for three marbles and two apples. All that could be seen of him in the dock, as the clerk read over the indictment, was his eyes and nose.

He was five-and-a-half years old.

Newgate Novelists

> On Sunday evenings the only books read were such as *Jack Sheppard, Dick Turpin,* and the *Newgate Calendar,* they got out of the neighbouring libraries by depositing 1*s*. These were read with much interest; the lodgers would sooner have these than any other books.
>
> *London Labour and the London Poor (1851)*

For a period of seventeen years, from 1830 to 1847, a group of novels was published having as a principal character a criminal who had been taken from the *Newgate Calendar,* or closely modelled on it. This caused the authors to be referred to as the 'Newgate novelists'; but it would be wrong from this to infer that there was a particular school to which they all belonged. Authors were beginning to see the possibilities of exploring the nature of criminality through their fiction, although the early attempts to do so inevitably bordered on farce.

One of the more ludicrous examples was the characterization of an Ordinary who assured a condemned man that when he went through the drop that he would be instantly lifted from the Old Bailey to Jerusalem! Others were more closely modelled on real personalities, such as the Regency murderer Thurtell, or the banker Henry Fauntleroy who had been hanged for forgery and whose stories had sold well in broadsheet and book form.

One of the 'Newgate novelists' was probably correct in saying that the true literature of Newgate was to be found in the daily newspapers. Certainly there was an enormous market in sensational literature which was considerably fuelled by the Seven Dials printers—such as Catnach and Pitts—who achieved what can only be considered as staggering sales with some of their broadsheets. These were hawked about the streets, sometimes on execution morning and sold to a sensation-hungry public—the broadsheet on Thurtell's execution sold more than one million. Earlier collections of the Ordinary's pamphlets were grouped together into various versions of the *Newgate Calendar,* which had developed on from the *Tyburn Chronicle* and *The Malefactors' Bloody Register,* the most popular being the Knapp and Baldwin edition and that of the Reverend Wilkinson.

The main exponents of the Newgate school were Bulwer-Lytton (*Eugene Aram*), Dickens (*Oliver Twist* and *Barnaby Rudge*), Harrison Ainsworth (*Rookwood* and *Jack Sheppard*) and lastly Thackeray (*Catherine*).

The greatest impact on the public mind was made by Harrison Ainsworth and Dickens. The former single-handedly in *Rookwood* created the legend of Dick Turpin and his ride to York, turning a rather commonplace Yorkshire butcher into the most famous highwayman of the road. It had been his intention to have completed a trilogy of such novels, with a major

296. Every Prisoner condemned to death shall be confined in some safe place within the Prison, apart from all other Prisoners, and shall be allowed such a dietary as the Visiting Justices may direct, and exercise in the open air for a reasonable time every day. He may be visited by his relations, friends, and legal advisers, at his own request, by an order in writing from any Visiting Justice. No other person shall have access to such Prisoner except the Governor, or other Officer of the Prison, the Ordinary, and Surgeon; or, if such Convict shall be of a religious persuasion differing from that of the Established Church, a Minister of that persuasion attending at his request. If any person, however, shall make it appear to a Visiting Justice that he has important business to transact with the Convict, such Visiting Justice may grant permission in writing to such person to have a conference with the Convict, in the presence of the Governor or an Officer appointed by him.

In all cases where sentence of death has been passed, and Convicts are left for execution, the Keeper

Newgate character in each, and in this way explore the themes of robbery in society, in Newgate and on the highway.

When the valet Courvoisier cut the throat of Lord William Russell, Ainsworth had to defend himself against the accusation that his second novel, *Jack Sheppard*, had inspired the murderer, only to have this confirmed by one of the sheriffs who had attended Courvoisier on the scaffold. The accusation was a disturbing one, though Ainsworth was publicly acquitted of intending or foreseeing the consequences of his writings, but the charge still remained that 'the admiration of the criminal is the studied purpose of the book'.

Significantly the third novel, with the highwayman Claude Duval as the central character, was never completed because of the rising hostility that was mounted against the Newgate 'school', partly on critical grounds, partly as a reaction against the loose-living of the Regency, and partly from a fear that the influence such books might have on the reading habits of the working classes might seep upwards into the higher strata of society. Ainsworth never again used a Newgate character as the central pivot of one of his stories.

Dickens never considered himself as a Newgate novelist. He regarded Ainsworth as an entertainer and himself as a moralist and put as much or Matron shall, immediately on their return to the Gaol, cause them to be thoroughly searched, and shall remove from them any instrument which may be considered either dangerous or inexpedient for them to retain on their person. The cell or room to which a Convict is reconducted after being sentenced to death shall immediately, on all such occasions, be previously examined by the Governor, who is to satisfy himself of its fitness and safety, and insert the result of his examination in his *Journal*. In all cases where sentence of death has been passed, and the condemned Prisoner left for execution, such Prisoner shall be placed under the constant superintendence of an Officer of the Prison by day and night.

———O———

Prisoners under sentence of death. From the Rules and Regulations for the Government of the Gaol of Newgate *(1873).*

distance as he could between them. Perhaps this can be better understood if one sees how they treated the grim stone prison itself. In Ainsworth's hands it is a cornerstone for romance with the great set-piece of Sheppard's escape over the roof. Dickens, in *Barnaby Rudge*, with its backdrop of the Gordon riots, uses it as a symbol of an oppressive social system together with the hangman who is similarly an instrument in the class struggle.

The controversies aroused by the Newgate novelists and their attacks on the harshness of the criminal laws, particularly that of capital punishment, were part of the class struggle between the have and have-nots (which Bulwer-Lytton coined) and were experimental in technique, reaching forward to the realism of a later age. In part the controversy was about whether there was a limit on the kind of material that was permissible for fiction and what exactly was the writer's responsibility and to whom. The Victorians 'respected art enough to be a little afraid of it. Some modern discussions of the freedom of the artist imply, by avoiding any consideration of the matter, that literature exercises no real influence upon thought and action. Such an attitude belittles the importance of imagination and of art. There is this to be said for Thackeray, Dickens, Bulwer, and all the Victorians, after an imbroglio deplorable, painful, and sometimes comic: they never doubted that the art of literature was an art of power.'

Gin and the pawnbroker

I have repeatedly observed, talking of the common Thieves, that they are born in a Crowd; they live in a Crowd; and they absolutely die in a Crowd; for they have no Time for Retirement, and what with living in a Crowd, and being perpetually half drunk, they have no Time to reflect, and of course they are ripe for any Depredation.

Evidence of the Rev Dr Cotton to the select Committee Inquiry into the present state of the several Gaols and Houses of Correction in England and Wales (1835)

In 1834 the number of prisoners awaiting trial at Newgate was increased when the jurisdiction of the Sessions House was extended to include not only London and Middlesex but the counties of Surrey, Essex and Kent. Prisoners were brought from these three counties on Saturday nights for trial on the Monday morning. Because of its increased jurisdiction the Sessions House was renamed and, with the addition of extra courts, became the Central Criminal Court. The number of sessions was increased from eight to twelve, which meant that the majority of prisoners were not held at Newgate before being sent to the transports or Houses of Correction for more than three weeks on average.

Because of the overcrowding which had continued for some years, the City had failed to implement the Gaol Act of 1825, partly as a way of insisting on its independence from government and partly because Newgate's construction did not allow for categorization or separation. In 1835 a Select Committee of the House of Lords was appointed to inquire into the state of gaols and Houses of Correction in England and Wales and the behaviour of other local authorities who, like the City, had failed to implement the Act either fully or in part. The prisons under the City's control—Newgate, the Giltspur Street Compter and the Borough Compter—were singled out for special mention as corrupting the morals of the inmates and tending to the extension rather than the suppression of crime. Evidence was collected not only from the establishment figures, such as Mrs Fry, Sir Peter Laurie and the prison officials, but from one of the turnkeys and two convicted men, one of whom was a wardsman.

Gin and the pawnbroker—so the keeper, Mr Cope, said—were the downfall of many of the prisoners. The prisoners' behaviour was as unchanged as ever: there was cursing, swearing, boasting of robberies, card-playing, pitch and toss, chuck-farthing, the singing of obscene songs and tales of porter and ale being bought and sold. One of the witnesses was a prisoner, Thomas Dexter, who had been sentenced to seven years transportation for stealing a 3s. pair of shoes when he was in great distress; he had been committed to Newgate in 1828.

On his first night the prisoners tried to levy their own brand of garnish, though this had supposedly been stopped ten years before; Dexter hit one of the men who was creeping up on him with a broom and was then left alone. Others had small things stolen from them such as handkerchiefs. He told the Select Committee that beer was brought in in buckets to be drunk when they were locked up for the night. By day there was little to do, and the Bible and prayer-book that were in the ward he had seen opened only once or twice. The Ordinary he had only seen once outside the chapel and that was when he brought a pair of shoes to him to be mended.

For a part of the time Dexter apparently had his family with him; one child died on the Friday night and the other on the Saturday morning. His wife was persecuted because of it as it was thought that they had died of gaol-fever. One can only assume that Sir Peter Laurie was being ironic when he told the same Committee of Inquiry: 'It is a common Remark, that if a Person wishes to be in Health, it would be well to send him to Newgate.'

Laurie's disapproval was chiefly for the wardsmen, who were selling bread and keeping back part of the meat ration to sell to other prisoners; the custom of letting friends bring in food had been discontinued and had been replaced by an increased prison allowance of one pound of potatoes to each prisoner every week. The wardsman, Edward Ingall, who gave evidence, confirmed that the bread was sold but tried to justify it by saying that the men were so ravenous that they would eat anything. He incurred the Committee's disapproval as well by his capitalistic behaviour in buying six mattresses and letting them out at 2s. or 2s. 6d. each week.. Wardsmen generally sold luxuries, such as tea, sugar, coffee and tobacco, and hired out knives, forks and plates. They had too much power and nobody to control them once the wards had been locked up for the night.

There were complaints that prisoners robbed each other and allegations of homosexual practices; one of the turnkeys thought there were no more than three to four incidents, which included the prison schoolmaster who had euphemistically taken 'liberties' with the boys. Other prisoners who did not participate in the ward rough and tumble were 'toed' by having cords tied to their feet and being dragged about the floor; they could be punished in other ways by having things stolen or burned. Sometimes the wardsmen could help the prisoners—if they had the skill—with the preparation of briefs and petitions, for which they would charge 1s. 6d. to 8s., depending on length. So absolute was the wardsman that the committee was told of one instance where a stabbing was reported to him rather than to the turnkey or keeper.

The same year Charles Dickens wrote on a visit to Newgate which was published in *Sketches by Boz*. He found in the men's wards an utter absence of employment:

Huddled together on two opposite forms, by the fireside, sit twenty men perhaps; here, a boy in livery; there, a man in a rough great-coat and top-boots; farther on, a desperate-looking fellow in his shirt sleeves, with an old Scotch cap upon his shaggy head; near him again, a tall ruffian, in a smock-frock; next to him, a miserable being of distressed appearance, with his head resting on his hand; – all alike in one respect, all idle and listless. When they do leave the fire, sauntering moodily about, lounging in the window, or leaning against the wall, vacantly swinging their bodies to and fro. With the exception of a man reading an old newspaper, in two or three instances, this was the case in every ward we entered.

Dietaries for prisoners. From the Rules and Regulations for the Government of the Gaol of Newgate *(1873).*

The following are the prescribed Rates of Diet.

CLASS I.

Convicted Prisoners confined for any term not exceeding Seven Days :—

MALES.	FEMALES.
Breakfast... Oatmeal gruel...1 pint.	Breakfast... Oatmeal gruel...1 pint.
Dinner...... Bread ....1 lb.	Dinner...... Bread ... .1 lb.
Supper...... Oatmeal gruel...1 pint.	Supper...... Oatmeal gruel ...1 pint.

CLASS II.

Convicted Prisoners for any term exceeding Seven Days and not exceeding Twenty-one Days:—

MALES.	FEMALES.
Breakfast... Oatmeal gruel... 1 pint.	Breakfast... Oatmeal gruel... 1 pint.
Bread .... 6 oz.	Bread .... 6 oz.
Dinner...... Bread............12 oz.	Dinner...... Bread .... 6 oz.
Supper ...... Oatmeal gruel... 1 pint.	Supper...... Oatmeal gruel... 1 pint.
Bread .... 6 oz.	Bread .... 6 oz.

Prisoners of this class, employed at hard labour, to have in addition 1 pint of soup per week.

CLASS III.

Convicted Prisoners employed at hard labour, for terms exceeding Twenty-one Days, but not more than Six Weeks; and Convicted Prisoners not employed at hard labour, for terms exceeding Twenty-one Days, but not more than Four Months:—

MALES.	FEMALES.
Breakfast... Oatmeal gruel... 1 pint.	Breakfast... Oatmeal gruel... 1 pint.
Bread .... 6 oz.	Bread .... 6 oz.
Wednesday and Friday.	*Wednesday and Friday.*
Dinner...... Soup ....1 pint.	Dinner...... Soup .... 1 pint.
Bread .... 8 oz.	Bread .... 6 oz.

MALES.	FEMALES.
Tuesday and Sunday.	*Tuesday and Sunday.*
Dinner......Cooked meat, without bone ... 3 oz.	Dinner......Cooked meat, without bone ... 3 oz.
Bread............... 8 oz.	Bread .... 6 oz.
Potatoes............ ½ lb.	Potatoes............ ½ lb.
Monday, Thursday, and Saturday.	*Monday, Thursday, and Saturday.*
Dinner...... Bread............... 8 oz.	Dinner...... Bread............... 6 oz.
Potatoes............ 1 lb.	Potatoes............ 1 lb.
or ½ pint of gruel when potatoes cannot be obtained.	or 1 pint of gruel when potatoes cannot be obtained.
Supper, same as breakfast.	Supper, same as breakfast.

CLASS IV.

Convicted Prisoners employed at hard labour, for terms exceeding Six Weeks, but not more than Four Months; and Convicted Prisoners not employed at hard labour, for terms exceeding Four Months:—

MALES.	FEMALES.
Breakfast... Oatmeal gruel... 1 pint.	Breakfast... Oatmeal gruel... 1 pint.
Bread .... 8 oz.	Bread .... 6 oz.
Sunday, Tuesday, Thursday, and Saturday.	*Sunday, Tuesday, Thursday, and Saturday.*
Dinner......Cooked meat, without bone ... 3 oz.	Dinner......Cooked meat, without bone ... 3 oz.
Potatoes......... ½ lb.	Potatoes............ ½ lb.
Bread............... 8 oz.	Bread .... 6 oz.
Monday, Wednesday, and Friday.	*Monday, Wednesday, and Friday.*
Dinner......Soup............... 1 pint.	Dinner......Soup............... 1 pint.
Bread .... 8 oz.	Bread .... 6 oz.
Supper, same as breakfast.	Supper, same as breakfast.

CLASS V.

Convicted Prisoners employed at hard labour, for terms exceeding Four Months:—

MALES.	FEMALES.
Sunday, Tuesday, Thursday, and Saturday.	*Sunday, Tuesday, Thursday, and Saturday.*
Breakfast... Oatmeal gruel... 1 pint.	Breakfast... Oatmeal gruel... 1 pint.
Bread .... 8 oz.	Bread .... 6 oz.

Cope was censured for his laxity in carrying out his responsibilities. He rarely visited the wards more than once or twice a week, instead of every twenty-four hours, and even these were curtailed because of his other duties. He used the turnkeys to clean his windows, stable and groom his horse (if necessary, for several hours a day), and they in turn did little more than count numbers and lock and unlock the wards which in turn devolved more power on the wardsmen. To make up the shortcomings in prison staff supervision Cope had closed some wards down completely and filled others to overflowing: prisoners were so tightly huddled together that on their tours of inspection the inspectors had great difficulty in picking their way in between them. Clothing was scarce. Some prisoners went barefooted and others had no soles to their boots. Generally they were dirty, unwashed and ragged.

In the women's yard Dickens saw a 'yellow, haggard, decrepit old woman, in a tattered gown that had once been black, and the remains of an old straw bonnet' talking to her daughter, 'a good-looking robust female, with a profusion of hair streaming about in the wind', and further on omitting every mention of the gates through which he passed and which would 'require a gate at every comma' he came to the school where was drawn up for his inspection fourteen young pickpockets.

> There was not one redeeming feature among them—not a glance of honesty—not a wink expressive of anything but the gallows and the hulks, in the whole collection. As to anything like shame or contrition, that was entirely out of the question. They were evidently quite gratified at being thought worth the trouble of looking at; their idea appeared to be, that we had come to see Newgate as a grand affair, and that they were an indispensable part of the show.

His opinion would have been echoed by the Rev Dr Cotton who thought that the juveniles went out worse than when they came in. For years he had tried to carry out his duties but had left off because he was interfered with and laughed at and was entirely frustrated in his efforts to achieve some reforms. Besides he was now too infirm to visit the prisoners in their cells or classes and they would normally see him only in chapel. In his opinion Newgate should be emptied of the boys and the women and used just for persons awaiting trial or execution.

The committee asked him bluntly: 'As a Place of Reformation do you consider that Newgate has no Claim?'

His answer was unequivocal: 'None upon earth.'

This highly critical inquiry forced the Corporation on to the defensive and in particular on charges that insane prisoners—there were seven, the longest had been at Newgate since 1831—mingled with the other prisoners, and that sexual offenders—meaning homosexual—mingled with the sexually inexperienced. They argued that prisoners had been returned from the asylums as being medically sane and boasted that they had escaped hanging by pleading insanity. They were on less sure ground with the second complaint but justified their decision not to put homosexuals into solitary confinement by saying that mixing with the other prisoners would stop them from indulging in former habits!

The report was dismissed as an exaggeration of isolated facts but it did force a number of minor changes on the prison. In their annual report the government inspectors continued to criticise the way that the prison was administered year by year. In their tenth annual report they were critical of the attempts to better ventilate the gaol with shafts sloping down to the slaughter-market behind it. This, in fact, only allowed the smell of rotting meat to drift through the system. There was also the added danger—because the pipe openings were so close to the ground—that rats could enter more freely into the prison.

Ultimately, it was only the completion of Holloway in 1852, and the change of use to a holding gaol for prisoners awaiting trial or under sentence of death, that closed these litanies of complaint and at the same time marked the beginning of the end for the centuries-old prison.

The Gallows

Considering the Number and Frequency of Executions in this metropolis, the almost infinite Multitudes that resort to these shocking Spectacles, with a kind of unnatural Eagerness, one would be tempted to imagine, that Hanging is become a Sport; and publick Justice executed on the most atrocious Criminals, is looked upon by the Inhabitants of the Cities of London and Westminster, as a mere Pastime. It is certain, the Design of executing Criminals in so publick a Manner, and with so much infamous Solemnity, is to strike a Terror upon the Minds of the People, and to give them a just Horror of the Crimes, that are attended with such dismal and shocking Consequences; the Government judging that such alarming Spectacles must sink deeper into the Minds, and have a more lasting Impression on the Dispositions of the Vulgar, than all the Lectures and Precepts of either Law or Religion . . . but either the Morals of the People are so much debauch'd, and their Hearts so hardened, that they cannot understand the Design of these Wretches being brought to suffer in their Sight; or Executions are become so frequent, that they have lost the Force of Novelty to make them operate on the Minds of the People, according to the wise Intention of the Legislature. Whatever is the reason, it is certain, these mournful and melancholy Scenes, have very little or no Effect upon the Morals of the People.

Memoirs of the Life of Mr James Maclean (1750)

As clever Tom Clinch, while the rabble was bawling,
Rode stately through Holborn to die in his calling,
He stopt at the George for a bottle of sack,
And promised to pay for it when he came back. . . .

Dean Swift, 'Clever Tom Clinch going to be hanged' (1727)

Hours have glided by, and still he sits upon the same stone bench with folded arms, heedless alike of the fast decreasing time before him, and the urgent entreaties of the good man at his side. The feeble light is wasting gradually, and the deathlike stillness of the street without, broken only by the rumbling of some passing vehicle which echoes mournfully through the empty yards, warns him that the night is waning fast away. The deep bell of St Paul's strikes—one! He heard it; it has roused him. Seven hours left! He paces the narrow limits of his cell with rapid strides, cold drops of terror starting on his forehead, and every muscle of his frame quivering with agony. Seven hours!

Charles Dickens, 'A Visit to Newgate'

Dead men

Have you ever taken any note of the proportion of felons condemned to
death who can read and write? No, never. I once had twelve people in the
condemned pew, as respectably dressed men to all appearance, as need to
be,; I should not have been ashamed to sit down with them at a public
table; and there was not one of them who knew how to open a book, or look
for a letter.

*Evidence of the Ordinary. Rev Brownlow
Ford, to the Committee on the State of
the Gaols of the City of London (1814)*

When asked what the prisoners' religious feelings were the Rev Cotton
could only reply 'Very dead'. This partly explains why, with his frustrations
over the school, he cut the daily services from two to one on Sundays and on
weekdays. After prayers had been said and he had visited the wards, he
managed to be free of his troublesome parishioners in under two hours
although he had no other duties to perform. His experiences were much the
same as his predecessor's, the Rev Brownlow Ford, who said that prisoners
never thought of prayers until the execution warrant was come and no felon,
but one who had been under sentence of death, had ever sent to him for
instruction. Sacraments were available only to those under sentence of
death and who expected to die within the week.

Services were held in the chapel—which was never full, although it could
accommodate only half the prison population. The exception was the
'Condemned' sermon which was preached on the Sunday before a hanging—then the chapel *was* full, with a good half of the space occupied by the
general public. The turnkeys charged admission fees to spectators, who
used it like a theatre; one of the beneficiaries was the City Swordbearer who
technically had the 'dwelling or keepership' of the Sessions House. The
Lord Mayor and sheriffs also charged fees for spectators in the galleries, but
in October 1774 the Swordbearer was forced to complain that at every
notable trial he found his gallery to be occupied by non-paying law students
who were eventually found a place near the jury. Between 1st August 1817
and 17th July 1818 the Swordbearer received a total of £604 11s. of which
more than half was from gallery fees. As more courts were added these fees
increased and it was not until 1860 that the practice was discontinued. How
much the turnkeys earned is not known but, the sermons being so popular,
they crammed in as many fee-paying persons as they could and, to make
more space, tried to turn away non-paying individuals, such as the Ordinary's wife on one occasion, who had a right to be present.

Part of the spectacle was the behaviour of the ordinary prisoners themselves, some of whom occupied two facing galleries, the women felons on
one side, debtors on the other. More were grouped downstairs about the

condemned pew in the centre of which, when there was to be a hanging, sat those who were to hang. They sat on either side of a black-painted coffin on a black, cloth-covered table. The galleries were even more like a theatre with the seats rising one above another. The chapel was lofty and cold and no fire burned there even in winter.

According to Brownlow Ford—and his evidence would have been echoed by past Ordinaries—the moment the women crowded into the gallery a dreadful row would begin, with 'hallooing and hooping, and calling to their old acquaintance' to know who was downstairs. When the Ordinary entered there would be a hush, but the moment that the blessing had been given the noise would start up again. Many of the prisoners were not only old acquaintances but some were on the same indictments and separated only because of their sex. The turnkeys and gatemen would try to keep order but, while they were speaking to one, others would be joking and laughing. Several times prisoners had been punished by being placed in solitary confinement from three to four hours, which could hardly have been more than a token penance. On one occasion, and Rev Brownlow Ford had never been able to find the culprit although he had offered a one-guinea reward, one of the prisoners had relieved himself only a few yards away from where he was standing and had done so in full view of the other prisoners, none of whom would give him away.

According to the keeper, Mr Brown, the number of prisoners fluctuated at the rate of 300 every six weeks. Out of 1375 convicted 81 were in the 10 to 14 years old category; 238 in the 14 to 18 years old category; and 211 in the 18 to 21 category; and of this number 108 had been sentenced to death. Most of these sentences were respited but for the others began the prelude to their deaths. The 'Condemned' sermon was compulsory attendance for them; the 'Condemned' pew was wainscotted in and they would sit around the black coffin, which they found a humiliating and shameful experience—every eye was upon them to see how much weight they had lost, whether their hair had changed colour, and to note how pale was their complexion. Some would adopt a swaggering bravado, others would genuinely join in the service and some would collapse or be in shock.

When Catherine Hayes was awaiting sentence in 1726 she and one of her two accomplices, Thomas Billings, caused great offence to the fee-paying public, by their behaviour, by holding hands and leaning on each other's shoulder for support. They had been convicted of murdering Catherine's husband; his head had been found on the Thames foreshore and put on a pole at Westminster for identification; it was this which led to the murderers' arrests. Mrs Hayes confession had pulled no punches. When asked why the murder had been committed she replied:

> Why, (said she), the Devil put it into my head! but, however, John Hays was none of the best of husbands, for I have been three parts starved ever since we were married together. I don't in the least repent of anything I

have done, but only in drawing those poor men into this misfortune. I was six weeks in importuning them to do it; they two or three times refused to be concerned in it; but at last I over persuaded them. My husband was made so drunk, that he fell out of his chair, and then they carried him into the back room, and laid him upon the bed, and there Billings knocked him on the head with a hatchet, and Wood cut his throat. This was what they told me, for I was not in the room when he was killed: But, as soon as he was dead, I went in and held the candle, while Wood cut his head quite off. But, says I, How came you to cut him and mangle him in such an inhuman manner? She answered, because we wanted to get him into a box; we thought to have done it with only cutting off his legs at the knees, but still we could not get him in, and therefore we cut off his thighs, and his arms, though when we had done, the box was too little to hold all, and shut close; and so the next night we put the body and limbs into two blankets, and Wood and Billings carried them away at twice, and threw them into a pond. But, says I again, What could induce the men to be guilty of all this? Was it the lucre of money? No, says she, there was nothing of that in the case, but the Devil was in us all, and we were all got drunk. . . . It will signify nothing to make a long preamble, I'll hold up my hand and confess myself guilty, for nothing can save me, and nobody can forgive me.

Catherine Hayes was burned for murdering her husband. He was killed with the help of two accomplices and the body dismembered.

The head was found and identified.

The executioner tried to strangle her before the flames reached the stake but burned his hands before he could do so.

The great mystery was the exact relationship between Hayes and Billings. It is more than probable that she was his mother and that the relationship was an incestuous one. This public demonstration of their affection for each other continued up to the moment of execution when Billings was hanged and Mrs Hayes chained to a stake, while brushwood was piled about her, and a running noose slipped about her neck. As the flames blazed up about her waist she tried to push the wood away; in the same instant the hangman jerked the rope to strangle her before the flames touched her flesh. Even then the flames were too quick for him and burned his hands, forcing him to drop the rope. More wood was hastily thrown onto the fire and in three to four hours time the body had been reduced to ashes.

Billings, meanwhile, had been cut down and hung in chains. The other accomplice, Wood, had died of gaol-fever four days before while lying in the Condemned Hold.

London of the gallows

After the executioner had tied her up I discovered a horrible dread in her countenance, and begged to know the cause. She said, 'I have many times passed by this place, and always when near it a dreadful horror seized me, for fear that one day I should be hanged; and this enters my mind afresh, and greatly terrifies me!'

The Life of Mr Silas Told (1786)

The first half of the eighteenth century saw a remarkable growth in the number of capital statutes. Acts which were passed as emergency measures to deal with local crises stayed unrepealed on the statute books. The most famous is the Act that was passed in 1722 which was 'An Act for the more effectual punishing wicked and evil disposed Persons going armed in Disguise, and doing Injuries and Violences to the Persons and Properties of His Majesty's Subjects, and for the more speedy bringing the Offenders to Justice'.

The short title is the Waltham Black Act and no other piece of legislation, before or since, has prescribed the death penalty for so many offences. According to the preamble it was aimed at persons who were going disguised (blacking their faces) and by modelling themselves on the Roberdsmen (the followers of Robin Hood) were committing similar outrages in the forests of Waltham, near Hampshire. The Act's original lifespan was supposed to be three years but it was continually prolonged, became a permanent enactment in 1757, and was not repealed until the next century.

Almost to the end of the seventeenth century it has been estimated that there were probably no more than fifty capital offences on the statute book. But this figure changes dramatically within a few years. Some idea of how great the change was can be gauged from the statistic that in the 300 years between the reigns of Edward III and Charles II only thirty-six capital statutes were enacted, while 187 capital statutes were passed from 1660-1819, so making it possible for a Member of Parliament to say in 1821:

> Men there are living, at whose birth our code contained less than seventy capital offences; and we have seen that number more than trebled. It is a fact that there stand upon our code one hundred and fifty offences, made capital during the last century. It is a fact that six hundred men were condemned to death last year upon statutes passed within that century. And it is also a fact, that a great proportion of those who were executed, were executed on statutes thus comparatively recent.

In 1833 a boy of nine was sentenced to death for poking a stick through a cracked shop window and stealing two pennyworth of paint. That was two years after another boy of nine was hanged at Chelmsford for setting fire to a house. Women were sometimes able to escape by 'pleading their belly'. The following was written in 1698.

> The Women or Wenches that are condemn'd to Death, never fail to plead they are with Child, (if they are old enough) in order to stop Execution till they are delivered. Upon this they are order'd to be visited by Matrons; if the Matrons do not find them Quick, they are sure to swing next execution-Day; but very often they declare that they are with Child, and often too the poor Criminals are so indeed; for tho' they came never so good Virgins into the Prison, they are a Sett of Wags there that take Care of these Matters. No Doubt they are diligent to inform them the very Moment they come in, that if they are not with Child already, they must go to work immediately to be so; that in case they have the Misfortune to be condemn'd, they may get Time, and so perhaps save their Lives. Who would not hearken to such wholesome Advice?

The increase in capital sentences was such that eighteenth-century London has been called the 'City of the Gallows'. Whether it was approached by road or by water a traveller could guarantee that at some point he would pass by a gibbet. Approaching it by river the traveller would pass by Execution Dock where pirates such as Captain Kidd were hanged until three tides had passed over them. By land the main crossroads into London had their own gallows, with Tyburn its most famous, until 1783.

In less than 150 years the number of offences for which a man could be hanged rose from 50 to more than 200. Many of these were added almost as an afterthought particularly in those bills dealing with the genesis of new manufacturing or trading industries. This was the only way, it was thought, that such industries could be protected. More perversely, although the number of capital offences increased—a man could be hanged for murder, for writing on Westminster Bridge, for stealing or for impersonating a Chelsea pensioner—the number of persons who were actually hanged did not. The figure more or less remained the same. Transportation was frequently substituted as a lesser punishment. Pardons were frequently used. This was a form of patronage which helped the property-owning classes to maintain their grip on employees who were too often referred to as the 'scum of the people' or more simply as 'the mob'.

'Tyburn Fair', which was how execution day was often viewed, was the catalyst for much of the mob violence. Executions had been carried out there since the twelfth century, but since 1571 a triangular-shaped gallows had been in use where the three roads met—the present-day Oxford Street, Edgware Road and Bayswater Road. The first man to die on it was a Catholic named John Storey. According to a contemporary pamphlet: 'The first day of June, the saide Storey was drawn upon a herdell from the Tower of London unto Tiborn, wher was prepared for him a newe payre of gallowes, made in triangular manner.' As the hangman was 'rifling among

Tiburn Road is present day Oxford Street and Tiburn Lane is now Park Lane. On the left is Hyde Park. Top left is the Tyburn gallows which used to stand almost opposite present day Marble Arch. The south-east leg was used to fix the boundary mark of St George's, Hanover Square. Below the gallows, at present day Speaker's Corner, is marked the place 'Where Soldiers are Shot'. From Rocque's Map of London, Westminster and Southwark *(1746).*

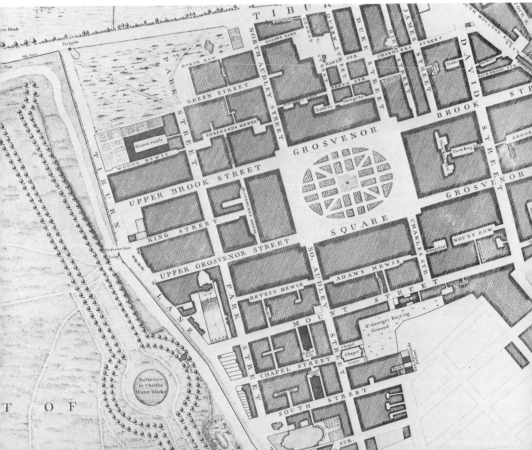

Oliver Cromwell's mummified head, which stood on the roof of Westminster Hall for over twenty years together with Bradshaw's and Ireton's who were treated in a similar manner. Their bodies were thrown into a pit under the Tyburn gallows.

his bowels', Storey rose up and struck him a blow. The gallows were eighteen feet high and triangular in shape so that eight people could be hanged from each beam at once, twenty-four at a time. At the Restoration the Cavaliers got their revenge on the Ironsides by digging up the bodies of Cromwell, Ireton and Bradshaw and hanging them in their shrouds from the gallows before cutting off their heads and spiking them on the roof of Westminster Hall. The bodies were thrown into a pit under the gallows.

The City from about 1570 onwards had its own Provost Marshal and marshalmen to co-ordinate its constables and watchmen against the growing menace of the beggars and the City's more unruly elements. Their orders were to hunt down and punish 'such notable rebellyous and incorrigible offenders worthilie to be speedilie executed by Marshalle Lawe to attach and take such personnes and in presence of the said Justices according to Justice of Marshalle Lawe to execute them uponn Galows or Gibbett . . .'. In 1595 after beggars had attacked a prisoner's escort the Provost Marshal, Sir Thomas Wilford, was given a portable gallows which he trundled about the City. Executions were carried out on this and other occasions at scattered spots throughout the City to ram the lesson home to the greatest number of spectators. Age was no barrier. In 1517 thirteen boys, some not in their teens, were hanged at Leadenhall, Newgate and Aldgate. Three hundred years later the Rev Dr Cotton told a Select Committee on Police in 1816 of four boys, aged between nine and thirteen years old, who between them had been in custody more than seventy times; the youngest had been abandoned when he was six and for the past three years had supported himself and his girl by begging and stealing; now aged nine, he was under sentence of death. Stow, in his history of the Ward of Aldgate, where he lived, describes how the Provost Marshal hanged a man for spreading rumours and at the same time vouches for the accuracy of the dying man's words by adding that the gallows was set up on the pavement outside his house.

At the execution of Colonel Turner in Leadenhall Street in 1663 there was a crowd of 20,000, among whom was Samuel Pepys—who got cramp in one leg from standing on a cart wheel for more than half an hour. According to a contemporary pamphlet, Turner was carted to the gallows and, calling the hangman to him, told him that his friends were desirous of having his clothes, which were part of the hangman's perquisites, but to compensate him for his loss they would pay him 50s. and give him 2s. 6d. extra for drink.

There was some impatience at the length of Turner's farewell speech and he had to be hurried up, but before concluding the Colonel made one last plea for the prisoners in Newgate. Turning to the sheriff he said:

> Sir, I must desire that you would now joyn with me in prayer, but I have forgot one thing, it is short; That night the Sessions broke up, I was put into the Hole, it is a most fearfull, sad, deplorable place, Hell itself in Comparison cannot be such a place, there is neither Bench, Stool nor Stick for any person there, they lye like swine upon the ground one upon another howling and roaring, it was more terrible to me than this Death; I would humbly begge that Hole may be provided with some kind of board like a Court of guard, that men may lye down upon them in ease, for when they should be best prepared for their ends, they are most tormented, lying only upon the ground, they were better take them and hang them as soon as they have their Sentence.

Ignoring the keeper's explanation that the reason why it was so bleak was because 'Seventeen out of nineteen made their escapes out of that Hole, they having only a Form there', Turner went on to say: 'I did with these poor Souls pray heartily; none were able to pray poor creatures, two were dying; I prayed with them, comforted them, assisted them, and gave them five shillings when I came out of the Hole.'

One of the main places of execution and pillorying was Smithfield, where cattle were bought and sold until 1853. In medieval times it was a popular place for jousting, but by the Elms which was where Wallace was hanged and quartered, several prisoners were boiled alive and the 'fires of Smithfield' raged in the Marian persecution. The usual spot for such burnings was in front of the gateway of St Bartholomew the Great. One of the first Protestants to be burnt as a heretic was the vicar of St Sepulchre's who had been kept in Newgate for some time amongst thieves and murderers. He was ordered to be burned in February 1555. As he was being dragged through Smithfield on a hurdle, 'his wife and children, eleven in number, ten able to go and one at the breast, met him as he passed. This sorrowful sight of his own flesh and blood could nothing move him, but that he constantly and cheerfully took his death with wonderful patience in the defence and quarrel of Christ's gospel.'

The burning of John Rogers, the Vicar of St Sepulchre's.

Ironically it became the subsequent custom for the bellman from his own church to exhort prisoners to repentance the night before they died. This custom originated in 1612 with a yearly bequest of £50 for the bellman to pronounce 'solemnly two exhortations to the persons condemned', once the night before they died and once again as they were carried past the church on their way to execution at Tyburn. The final form of these verses was as follows:

> All you that in the condemned hole do lie,
> Prepare you, for tomorrow you shall die;
> Watch all and pray; The hour is drawing near.
> That you before the Almighty must appear.
>
> Examine well yourselves; in time repent.
> That you may not to eternal flames be sent.
> And when St Sepulchre's Bell in the morning tolls.
> The Lord above have mercy on your souls.
> PAST 12 O'CLOCK.

The bellman of St Sepulchre's.

The execution handbell of St Sepulchre's church.

Newgate notorious

Robbing is the only thing that goes on with any vivacity, though my friend Mr M'Lean is hanged. The first Sunday after his condemnation, three thousand people went to see him; he fainted away twice with the heat of his cell. You can't conceive the ridiculous rage there is of going to Newgate; and the prints that are published of the malefactors, and the memoirs of their lives and deaths set forth with as much parade as—as—Marshal Turenne's. WE have no Generals worth making a parallel.

Horace Walpole Letters

Once they had been sentenced to death, condemned prisoners could be put on show if they were particular money-makers. The turnkeys earned several hundreds of pounds out of Sheppard by charging 3s. 6d. viewing fee. Sheppard was not averse to this adulation; Defoe wrote his life and Thornhill painted his picture. Three thousand people came to see the highwayman M'Lean who had not only held Walpole up but had shot him in the face. The heat was so great that M'Lean fainted.

Almost any excess was tolerated. Sixteen String John Rann (so-called because he wore eight silk strings at each knee) had seven women to dine with him three days before he was hanged and was, so it was reported, extremely cheerful. More remarkable still was the behaviour of 'The Monster', Renwick Williams, who had acquired his exaggerated reputation by stabbing but only wounding his victims; he had forty friends and fellow-prisoners to tea, which was followed by dancing and a cold supper and a general dispersal at 9 p.m. when the prison gates were locked.

It was customary to invite the Ordinary to supper the night before execution. On one such occasion a visitor overheard someone ordering a boiled chicken for a prisoner that was to be executed next morning. The gaoler added that the turnkey needn't be too particular about the sauce. 'That is true, says the other, but the Ordinary sups with him, and you know he is a hell of a fellow for butter!'

Other prisoners remained in a state of shock throughout the night. Silas Told, who was a Methodist preacher and visitor to Newgate for over twenty-one years (circa 1754 to 1775) despite the animosity from the keepers and the Ordinary, said of one prisoner that he came out of his cell like a man deprived of his senses and in chapel became so violent that the Ordinary ran away.

This was the last occasion that the final sacrament was given to the prisoners, though it could be refused, as it was to Thomas Milksop in 1722 because he could not remember how many murders and robberies he had committed. The Ordinary (Lorrain) possibly wanted the details for his pamphlets but Milksop defiantly told him 'that if he was not allowed to go to heaven with the others, he would try to find out the way by himself'. The

'Flying Highwayman', William Hawke, came down with the other prisoners on the morning of 1st July 1774, at seven o'clock exactly, having spent the night in their company singing psalms and praying. One of his accomplices was trembling 'as if his frame was dissolving', but Hawke's composure remained unbroken even when he reached the gallows and saw the waiting hearse bearing a black coffin with yellow nails, on which was already attached the engraved plate with his name and date of dying.

Tyburn Fair

Some who hear me are perhaps blaming the judges, the jury and the hangman; but neither the judge, jury nor hangman are to blame: they are but ministerial agents; the true hangman is the member of parliament; he who frames the bloody law is answerable for all the blood that is shed under it.

Sir William Meredith, *Parliamentary Debates (1777)*

'When the Day of Execution is come, among Extraordinary Sinners, and Persons condemned for their Crimes, who have but that Morning to live, one would expect a deep Sense of Sorrow, with all the Signs of a thorough Contrition', wrote Mandeville in 1725, but was forced to conclude 'the very Reverse is true'. Throughout the gaol nothing can be heard but the howling of voices, turnkeys bellowing names, the clanking of chains (the sound varying on their weight), quarrelling, loud laughter, shouts for more beer and the answering cries of the tapsters; the ribaldry, the mad drinking, the crying of the penitent and the jeering of the impudent, whilst throughout this bustle moved the Ordinary offering scraps of consolation to unattentive listeners. One of his successors, in the nineteenth century, said that in his twelve years' experience he could not remember a single instance of genuine conversion—except to prisoners who were about to be executed.

For many of the prisoners the moment that they had dreaded so much must have come as some sort of relief: this would have been the first time that some of them would have stood in daylight for possibly several weeks. In the Press Room their irons were struck off, and their elbows pinned from behind, which left their hands free to clasp a friend's hand, fold in prayer, swallow a last drink or catch hold of the body nearest to them, as Wild did, when the hangman whipped up his horse and the cart pulled away. With some of the prisoners extra security meant that the handcuffs were left on. Sheppard was one of those who swore and cursed the sheriff when he would not remove his irons. This so aroused suspicions that the sheriff ordered him to be searched again. As the turnkey ran his hands over his clothes he cut his hand on a concealed knife which Sheppard had ready to cut his ropes with before trying to escape into the crowd where it was thickest.

Before mounting the cart, which was sometimes draped in black, a noose was hung about each prisoner's neck. At this some of the prisoners would crack under the strain. Fifteen-year-old Joseph Harris, who was hanged for stealing two half-sovereigns and some silver at the same time as Dr Dodd, had to be lifted into the cart and rode with his head in his father's lap. His father stayed with him until the hangman turned him off, the crowd openly sympathizing with the grey-haired old man who was weeping the whole time.

Most prisoners tried to cover their fears with shows of finery, some wearing their best clothes, some with white caps and black ribbons. As the bellman intoned his set of verses for the second time others caught hold of the nosegays thrown to them by the young girls outside St Sepulchre's, putting them in their shirt fronts as buttonholes or holding them in their hands.

Not all the prisoners rode in carts. Those who were sentenced for treason were dragged backwards on a hurdle to Tyburn with the sheriffs' officers, swords drawn, facing them on the tailboard, their weight anchoring the hurdle to the ground. Others, who could afford it, rode in their own or hired coaches while yet others rode in the carts sitting on their coffins. The Ordinary, or a chaplain of their choosing such as Silas Told, would ride with them, reading prayers and exhorting them to higher thoughts.

Inevitably there were exceptions. The Rev Villette's behaviour to Dodd was one of 'boorish indifference'. His only interest in the prisoners seems to have been that of extracting more details for the broadsheet that he was writing up for publication at 6d. a time. In manner he is similar to Lorrain. Once he tried to hamper the last-minute reprieve on the gallows of a young boy who had been wrongly sentenced to death for a crime which someone else had confessed to; the boy was reprieved despite Villette's angry bullying of the hangman whom he told to get on with it as it was too late now to worry about such details! His *Annals of Newgate* (1773) was simply a compilation of the work of former Ordinaries which he published without any form of acknowledgment as to source.

Even in the carts there was a rule of precedence. The first two ranks went not to those convicted of murder but first to those who had robbed the mail and next to the highwaymen. On either side of the carts the escort would form up: this consisted of the City Marshal, Under Marshal, marshalmen, javelin men and constables—about 200 strong. Somewhere, among the leading carts, would be the hangman. On one occasion the whole procession came to a crushing halt when the hangman, William Marvell, was arrested and the three men he was to have hanged were returned to Newgate and pardoned!

Dr Archibald Cameron being drawn on a hurdle to Tyburn. He was hanged, drawn and quartered on 7 June 1753 for High Treason.

As soon as the condemned carts swung through the gate into the street the crowd boiled up about them; mostly they were working-class people and a strong element of the underworld. For anyone who had their hatred it was a fearsome experience and not even the presence of the chaplain in the same cart could protect them from the crowd's wrath. Mrs Brownrigg was hanged in 1767 for the brutal murder of her apprentice. Told, who accompanied her, wrote that after he had stationed himself he 'perceived the whole powers of darkness ready to give her a reception'. Inside the prison the crowd fell silent when he asked them to pray for her, but outside it was a

Mrs Brownrigg whipping her apprentice Mary Clifford. The devil urges her on by saying 'Go on and prosper and remember I am your friend'.

different story—the road on either side was lined with carts of women who shouted: 'Pull off her hat that we may see the bitch's face', threw stones, dirt, shouted and screamed, and even when she was tied up showed little or no compassion.

There was the same lack of compassion when Barbara Spencer was burned for uttering false coins in 1721. When tied to the stake 'she was very desirous of praying, and complained of the dirt and stones thrown by the mob behind her, which prevented her thinking sedately on futurity. One time she was quite beat down by them .'

In his heyday Wild, who was equally hated, would mock the prisoners by riding ahead of the carts, and with the greatest glee imaginable, would tell people that his 'children' were coming, they were just behind. So, when he made the same journey, several thieves went ahead of him telling the people that their 'father' was coming, he was just behind. Knowing what he had to face Wild tried to commit suicide but took too large a dose of laudanum and threw most of it up. When he climbed into the cart next morning, in a nightgown and linen headcloth, to a great shout from the crowd, he was still suffering both from its effects and the cut throat inflicted by Blueskin Blake when he had tried to take off his head. On the way to Tyburn his head was cut with stones and the hangman almost attacked for not dispatching him so quickly as the others.

Thieves and pickpockets of both sexes swarmed along the route. The mob was a safeguard of sorts to the thieves who would normally have stayed away, but as execution day was well known beforehand, it was tantamount to giving them a general amnesty. 'All the Way, from Newgate to Tyburn, is one continued fair, for Whores and Rogues of the meaner Sort. Here the most abandon'd Rakehells may light on Women as shameless! Here Trollops, all in Rags, may pick up Sweethearts of the same politeness; And there are none so lewd, so vile or so indigent, of either Sex, but at the Time and Place aforesaid, they may find a Paramour.'

All the time there was a constant thrust and jostle of people, with men and women being tumbled in the mud, the fine suits of the young rake-hells who had debauched the night away being spoiled by the carcases of mud-trampled dogs and cats whistling through the air wherever the crowd was thickest, the raucous cries of the gin-sellers with bottles of raw spirits in their baskets—which steadily emptied as they kept pace with the procession, and the constant hubbub of shouting as the procession drew nearer to Tyburn.

For those in the carts the journey could take up to three hours. By then, no matter how much they had drunk, the worse effects were beginning to wear off or would have done had the carts not stopped at least three or four times to let them buy more alcohol. A story, common to several executions, is of the condemned man calling for a pint of brandy and promising to pay for it—when he came back!

As clever Tom Clinch, while the rabble was bawling,
Rode stately through Holborn to die in his calling,
He stopt at the George for a bottle of sack,
And promised to pay for it when he came back.

At such stops the crowds would push through the escort to shake hands with the more celebrated criminals. Even worse crowds were waiting at Tyburn where stands had been erected since 1724 at the latest to give a better view. These pews resembled a modern race-course stand. Most of them were destroyed in a riot that followed the reprieve of a man who was to have been hanged for treason in 1758. They must have been immediately rebuilt, as the owner of the plot of ground on which they stood earned herself more than £5,000 when Earl Ferrers was executed on the first drop. The owner was the widow of a cowkeeper named Proctor, which led to a number of the seats being popularly known as 'Mother Proctor's Pews'.

Mandeville was appalled by the fights that increased in ferocity between the escort and the crowd as it fought to get through. Heads were broken, sticks swung and blood flowed as the carts pushed their way steadily towards the eighteen-foot-high triangular-shaped gallows and the half moon of seats rising in tiers to a great height behind it. Some of the more enterprising spectators had brought ladders which they would hire out at so many rungs for persons who wanted a good view. Mingling with the great crowd were horsemen and hackney coaches, all dirty and covered with dust, with the occupants shouting or abusing each other, while at the foot of the gallows waited the friends ready to pull on the legs that would soon be dangling at the ends of ropes.

The crowd brought out the worst elements of London life. Mingling with the merely curious were pickpockets, thieves, prostitutes, drunkards, the ballad sellers, the hot pies man, and the gingerbread man Tiddy Dol. As the disorders increased, a file of soldiers stationed around the gallows to keep order became a permanent part of the proceedings as 'the nubbing cheat', 'the three-legged mare', the 'deadly nevergreen' took its fatal toll.

The Tyburn spectators were hardened to what they saw. There was no drop and no dislocation of the neck. As the hangman's cart pulled away the bodies would swing off the tailboard and strangle at the end of a thin rope. Sometimes the prisoners would try to hasten the process as did the high-wayman James MacLean who kicked off his shoes and jumped into the air hugging his knees to his chest. Usually friends would be standing by to pull on the legs or beat the chest until death intervened. Death was an accepted fact. 'A man will piss when he cannot whistle', was one popular saying. Another was, more fatalistically, 'that there is nothing in being hang'd but a wry Neck, and a wet pair of Breeches'.

Jonathan Wild on his way to execution. He is sitting in the cart while directly behind him is the bellman of St Sepulchre's.

William Hogarth's The Idle Apprentice Executed at Tyburn. *Notes: The hangman is sitting astride the top beam of the gallows smoking a pipe; the preacher is exhorting the condemned man to repentance who is leaning against his coffin; on the right are the stands that were put up for spectators to get a better view; in the foreground is a ballad seller selling* The Last Dying Speech and Confession

Jack Ketch

I was there on duty, and I noticed particularly two costermongers who were proceeding to the execution, they were going up Snowhill, I believe, and one said to the other, 'So help me God, Bill aint it fine, five of them and all darkies'. The answer of the other man was 'It is so, and I should like to act Jack Ketch to them . . .'.

Evidence of Inspector Thomas Kittle who
was referring to the execution of five
pirates in 1864 when he gave evidence to
the Commission on Capital Punishment (1866)

The name of Jack Ketch is a synonym for hangmen in general. The original Ketch was hangman from 1663 to 1686, when he was turned out in the January because he had insulted one of the sheriffs. But he had to be reinstated only four months later because his successor had been hanged for stealing! He died in November that same year leaving behind him a reputation for butchery and incompetence that was never surpassed before or since. The poet John Dryden was being satirical when he wrote: 'A man may be capable as Jack Ketch's wife said of his servant, of a plain piece of work, a bare hanging, but to make a malefactor die sweetly was only belonging to her husband.' His reputation has only been equalled by that of the nineteenth-century hangman, William Calcraft, of whom it was said that if he was hanging a dog he would be just the same.

In his last year much of his posthumous reputation was acquired because of his bungling of the Duke of Monmouth's execution. Monmouth, however craven he had been before, was calm enough on the day but, feeling the axe, doubted if it was sharp enough. However, he seemed satisfied when Ketch assured him that it would be both sharp enough and heavy enough. Handing Ketch six guineas to make him strike harder Monmouth laid his head on the block and waited for the blow. As he had supposed, the axe was blunt. Ketch hit him five times without taking off the head.

Wrote a contemporary:

The executioner struck an agitated blow, inflicting a small cut, and Monmouth staggered to his feet and looked at him in silent reproach. Then he resumed his place and the executioner struck him again and again. Still the head remained on the block, while his body writhed in agony. As the horrified fury of the crowd increased the headsman flung down the axe, crying out: 'I cannot do it. My heart fails me.' 'Take up the axe, man', roared the Sheriff, while the crowd cried, 'Fling him over the rails!' So he took it up again and hacked away, but the job had to be finished with a knife. A strong guard protected him as he went off, else he would have been torn to pieces.

Some weeks later he was down in the west country carrying out the executions of Monmouth's supporters, those who had been sentenced in the Bloody Assizes; even with the butcher he had brought from London to help him he found it physically impossible to hang, draw and quarter more than thirteen persons in one day let alone the twenty-five that had been sentenced in the first batch of judicial killings. This is the warrant that was given by the Sheriff of Somerset, and must have been typical of many, to the constables of Bath where four rebels were to be executed:

> These are therefore to will and require you immediately on sight hereof to erect a gallows in the most public place of yor said cittie to hang the said traytors on, and that you provide halters to hang them with, a sufficient number of faggots to burne the bowels of fower traytors and a furnace or cauldron to boyle their heads and quarters, and salt to boyle therwith, half a bushell to each traytor, and tarr to tarr them with and a sufficient number of spears and poles to fix and place their heads and quarters, and that you warne the owners of fower oxen to bee ready with a dray or wayne and the said fower oxen at the time hereafter mencioned for execution, and yourselves togeather with a guard of fortie able men att the least, to be present on Wednesday morning next by eight of the clock, to be aiding and assisting to me, or my deputie, to see the said rebells executed.

They were 'also to provide an axe and cleaver for the quartering of the said rebels'.

By the time this bloody work was finished the west country stank with the smell of rotting flesh: there they hung for nearly a year, on gates, bridges and other places, some 250 pickled heads and 1,000 mutilated quarters.

This part explains why, when Ketch died the following year, his name became synonomous with hangmen generally. Others, equally brutal, were similarly prepared to mangle a man's limbs for just a few pence. There was a popular saying at one time that the worse thing you could do to a man was to hang him and the next to make him hangman. Perhaps it should be pointed out that there has never been such an official as the 'hangman of England'. Until this century the best known was the hangman appointed by the City of London. As transport became quicker, and the number of capital sentences fewer, it was found generally cheaper to hire him for such occasions rather than have a permanent appointment.

Sometimes the hangman could fall on lean times. In 1706 Richard Pearse petitioned the Court of Aldermen for something to keep himself from starving 'he being ffitt for no other imployment . . .'. Another hangman refused to whip some offenders unless his wages were increased; he complained 'for many months I have had no jobs but whipping and that puts nothing in a man's pocket . . . and if it wasn't for a hanging job now and then in the country, where there's few in my line, I should likely have been quite ruined. I used to get clothes; and very often some gentleman would tip me a few guineas for civility, before he was turned off.'

In an effort to impart some dignity to the office, one of the sheriffs gave the eighteenth-century hangman, Edward Dennis, a splendid robe which he instantly converted into cash because it was far too cumbersome to wear. He was sentenced to hang for taking part in the Gordon Riots but was reprieved so that he could hang his fellow rioters.

After he had hanged the 'Flying Highwayman', William Hawke, he turned up at the impressive church service that was given at the burial at Uxbridge, with nearly the whole town present, as one of the principal mourners! The Jacobean hangman, Gregory Brandon (his son Richard, as a boy, practised cutting off cats' heads and is thought to have been the masked man who beheaded Charles I), was jokingly given a coat-of-arms by the College of Heralds and ever afterwards referred to as Brandon Esquire.

Sometimes at executions the hangman was drunk. In 1738 he was so befuddled that he not only put the nooses on the two house-breakers he was about to hang but tried to slip one on the Ordinary who was praying with them! Worse still, though more understandable, was the behaviour of the Irish woman, Hannah Dagoe, who put up such a fierce fight, got her arms free and punched the hangman so hard that she nearly knocked him out of the cart and *dared* him to hang her. So that he wouldn't have her clothes, which were part of his customary perquisites, she tore them off and flung them into the crowd. When at last the rope was got about her neck she flung herself out of the cart so hard that she managed to break it.

Sometimes the roles were reversed and the hangman himself made victim. Two of the earliest hangmen to be identified, one by his name and the other by his deformity, were hanged within a few years of each other. The former was a hangman named Cratwell and the other, described as he went to execution in 1556, is referred to simply as 'the hangman with the stump leg'.

John Price (1714-15) earned the dubious distinction of being 'the hangman who was hanged and gibbeted afterwards'. Convicted of the murder of an old woman gingerbread seller he was hanged in 1718. The iron suit that was made for him to be gibbeted was forged by his successor, William Marvell, who was arrested for debt when he was on his way to Tyburn to hang three men. The bailiff, who had served the writ, was satisfied now that it had been served to let him continue, but instead the mob beat Marvell into unconsciousness. The same thing happened to the bricklayer who offered to double up for him. The three prisoners were taken back to Newgate, subsequently reprieved and their sentences commuted to life imprisonment. Marvell was sacked from his job as 'Executioner-General of Great Britain' (a self-styled title which has echoes of Wild). Two years later he was convicted of theft and transported.

More fortunate still was the Elizabethan hangman, Derrick, who was sentenced to death for rape but saved by the intervention of his patron the Earl of Essex. He repaid the favour by beheading him for treason several years later. Derrick's posthumous fame still survives today. The modern derrick crane is named after the design of his gallows. This suggests that instead of using a primitive form of drop, such as a cart's end, he winched his victims into the air.

One of the hangman's perquisites was the clothes of the persons he hanged, which he could sell for their value. Three Sundays after Dr Dodd's execution the clerk of the chapel where he used to preach was seen in the black suit that he had worn for his hanging. Earl Ferrers, who blamed his misfortunes on his marriage, went to the gallows, after murdering his steward, in the same white suit richly embroidered in silver in which he had been married. Others dressed in white or wore a white cockade in their hats to protest their innocence. Some, such as Wild, who went to execution in his night shirt, and Stephen Gardner, a highwayman, who was hanged in 1724, wore a shroud, dressed so as to cheat the hangman. Possibly, in Gardner's case, the shroud might have been worn as a sign of genuine penitence but this seems doubtful.

Between June and October 1759 the old, permanently fixed, triangular gallows which had been in use for over 200 years was dismantled and replaced with a portable one which could be brought with the prisoners on carts on execution day and easily assembled. According to the *Whitehall Evening Post* of 4th October 1759: 'Yesterday morning, about Half an Hour after Nine o'clock, the four malefactors were carried in two carts from Newgate, and executed on the new Moving Gallows at Tyburn. . . . The Gallows, after the Bodies were cut down, was carried off in a cart.' The timber from the old bloodstained triple tree was sold to a carpenter who cut it down and turned it into beer-butt stands for the cellar of the 'Carpenters' Arms' public house close by.

A few months later, in May 1760, Earl Ferrers was executed on the new drop. His procession to Tyburn was an elaborate affair. He rode in a landau rather than the more appropriately named mourning coach, with the Ordinary and one of the sheriffs for company; the latter politely observed that he would try to render his situation as agreeable as possible! The crowds were so dense that it took nearly three hours to reach the fatal tree. Ferrers thought that passing through such crowds was ten times worse than death itself.

The execution was doubly unique in that not only was it the first time that a drop was used but also that a peer of the realm was being hanged, rather than beheaded, as was customary. Because of the crowds the gallows was surrounded by a strong force of Horse Grenadiers and Foot Soldiers. Instead of the old triangular gallows being used, a new scaffold had been built nearby for the occasion with a single beam and a railed-in platform with ornamental black bays. Black cushions had been provided for Ferrers and the Ordinary on which to kneel for the final prayers.

When the moment came Ferrers pulled a white cap from his pocket,

The execution of Earl Ferrers was the first time that a drop was used.

Earl Ferrers as he lay in his coffin at Surgeon's Hall.

which he pulled down over his face, his arms were tied with a black sash and the halter—hemp and not silk as is often alleged—was placed about his neck. The drop was not a trapdoor but a small platform only eighteen inches above the main platform level and far too low to allow for any dislocation of the neck. When the signal was given the hangman knocked away the pegs, the drop fell and Ferrers was strangled to death. Because the rope had not been stretched, as happens with modern hangings, Ferrers' feet still brushed the ground. He struggled for a few moments and then had to be finished off, as a contemporary pamphlet puts it, 'by the pressure of the executioner'.

The body was taken to Surgeon's Hall for dissection in a coffin lined with white satin, his hat and the halter curled at his feet. On the lid had been put, prophetically, a coffin plate marked 'Laurence Earl Ferrers, suffered May 5, 1760'.

The only unseemly note to mar the occasion was the hangman's wrangling with his assistant, moments before the execution, because Ferrers by mistake had given the five guineas for a swift death to the assistant and not to Ketch himself. So incensed was the hangman by this that until it was settled he refused to proceed with the execution!

Body-snatching

The method of falling should be secured if the executioner does his duty; but the weight of the body will have a great effect, and the state of the man at the time; if he can stand up so as to have a greater fall, and the rope has a long bend, the jerk will almost always have its effect more quickly than where the man is short, and the rope consequently, has a less fall.

Evidence of City Police Superintendent, Charles Hodgson, to the Select Committee Inquiry To Take into Consideration the present Mode of carrying into effect Capital Punishments (1856)

One reason for so much turbulence and disorder at the hangings was the fights that frequently took place for possession of the body. It was only in the seventeenth and eighteenth centuries that surgery, as we understand it, began to make its spectacular advances. Before then the church had frowned on dissection as an act of blasphemy towards God.

Behind the Sessions House was Surgeon's Hall. After execution the bodies were brought here and publicly dissected in front of fee-paying spectators who were given a course of three-day lectures which concluded with a banquet at which the subject was the chief topic of discussion. After

Left: *The dissection room at Surgeon's Hall. In the alcoves are the dissected skeletons of persons who had been hanged.*

The skeleton of Mrs Brownrigg in Surgeon's Hall.

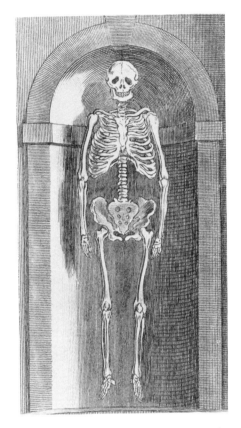

anatomization the articulated skeletons were hung in alcoves about the dissection room.

By law the surgeons were allowed only ten bodies every year. The Royal College of Physicians was allowed the bodies of 'One or Six persons condemned to Death within London, Middlesex or Surrey for anatomical Dissection', and the Barber-Surgeons four. None was allowed to the private hospitals and medical schools who had to turn to other sources. This meant that there was a great trade in grave-robbing and body-snatching generally. It was this which caused the fights as friends and family fought the surgeon's agents for possession of the corpse. Law was on the side of the surgeons. For trying to rescue a body the punishment was seven years' imprisonment. Sometimes the struggle was so fierce that people were killed and, by one of those ironic twists of fate, could sometimes send one of the rescuers to the same gallows several weeks later.

A certain amount of dealing went on before the execution, sometimes with the prisoner who wanted some money for himself or his family, and sometimes with the hangman for the clothes and/or body. Because of the value of some of the prisoners' clothes—they would dress as if for a wedding—there was an added incentive to strip the body before handing it over.

The great dread for many was not so much the hanging—'It is nothing, it is only a kick'—but what was to be done to their body after death. Many of them had their families with them in their last moments to offer comfort and the promise of a Christian burial; they did not want to be mangled and anatomized or, like Wild, who was dug up by body-snatchers, have their body filleted and the flesh dumped on some foreshore.

As if death was not sufficient enough the law inflicted still further punishment. To intensify still more the public horror of dissection an Act to aggravate the death penalty was passed in 1752. This was popularly known as the 'Murder Act' but its correct title was 'An Act for better preventing the horrid Crime of Murder'. Henry Fielding, the novelist and magistrate, was one of the prime movers behind it. He was anxious for the Tyburn procession to be abolished as well as public executions, believing that these should be done in private. The main clause of the Act was that no murderer should be buried until after the body had been dissected and exposed to public view. As this coincided with the interests of the surgeons the Act had their total support. The Ordinary found divine justification for dissection in the Book of Genesis where God repented of making man and sent a flood to cover the earth. The first person to be sentenced under the new Act 'was taken from the bar weeping and in great agonies, lamenting his sad fate'.

Part of this fear can be attributed to the crowd's belief in 'resurrection' or, in modern terms, resuscitation. Because death was not instantaneous from a broken neck there had been many instances of bodies being cut down and successfully revived even though they may have hung for half an hour or more. In Tudor times 'resurrections' were so frequent that the Barber-Surgeons ordered that the persons who brought them the bodies should be charged the incidental expenses. One possible explanation is that the hangman may have been bribed as to where exactly he positioned the knot or, the alternative, that friends were sometimes supporting and not always pulling on the legs. In 1740 William Duell was one of five men hanged at Tyburn. The *Gentleman's Magazine* reported:

> The body of this last was brought to Surgeon's Hall to be anatomiz'd; but after it was stripped, and laid on the board, and one of the Servants was washing him, in order to be cut, he perceiv'd Life in him, and found his Breath to come quicker and quicker; on which a Surgeon took some Ounces of Blood from him; in two Hours he was able to sit up in his Chair, and in the Evening, was again committed to Newgate.

He was kept at the Surgeon's Hall until midnight and allowed to gradually come to. He could not speak and was understandably in a distressed condition. Next day he had recovered his voice and asked to see his mother; while waiting he ate a good meal. His sentence was commuted to transportation for life.

In 1709 an ex-soldier, John Smith, was hanged for burglary but had only been dangling for about five minutes when a belated reprieve came for him. He was instantly cut down and soon recovered. When asked his sensations he replied that 'at first he felt great pain, but that it gradually subsided, and that the last thing he could remember, was the appearance of a light in his eyes, after which he became quite insensible. But the greatest pain was, when he felt the blood returning to its proper channels.' As a result of his experience he became known as 'Half-Hanged Smith'. His experience was similar to John Hayes in 1782 who 'thought I was in a beautiful green field and that is all I remember till I found myself in the dissecting room'. Another victim of the scaffold is reported as having thrust back the lid of his coffin and pulled himself up to the astonishment of all the spectators. The hangman was all for starting again but the crowd would not let him and carried the 'body' off. Sad to relate that despite their efforts he died before they reached town.

Friends' efforts to bribe the hangman were buttressed in some cases with elaborate arrangements for a speedy resurrection once the body had been cut down. Sheppard's friends had hot blankets and a surgeon ready to attempt resuscitation. When Dr Dodd was cut down 'Air mixed with "volatile alkali" was pumped into the Doctor's lungs by a double-bellows, spirits of hartshorn being held in front of the bellows air-inlet. His spine and oesophagus were pressed and massaged. Blankets had to be held in such a way that they hardly touched him, while steam of hot balsam was circulated round his body and forced up his anus. Peppermint water, horseradish juice and turpentine were applied, but all in vain.'

Until the passing of the 'Murder Act' in 1752, the struggle under the gallows continued. The hangman continued to be bribed with money and clothes or had to be compensated for injuries and lost earnings. The difficulty of getting cadavers meant incidental expenses, such as broken windows, wrecked coaches and compensation for personal injuries. All this changed literally overnight with the passing of the Act.

More bodies were now available for dissection and the shambles at Tyburn Fair did not have to take such an extreme form.

Mandeville was just one of many who was highly critical of the 'Tyburn Fairs'. Fielding was another, and in his 'Enquiry into the Cause of the late increase of Robbers' made the point: 'The day appointed by law for the thief's shame is the day of glory in his own opinion.' In his view execution should follow quickly after sentence before the initial horror at the crime had had time to evaporate into pity for the condemned man. To heighten the effect and to make a much more horrifying impression the execution should be in private. This view was in sharp conflict with the official one that open executions were the greater deterrent and that the more people who witnessed them the greater the salutary effect. Such a view-point had the sturdy support of Dr Johnson. To the objection that it drew together a number of spectators he replied: 'Sir, executions are intended to draw spectators. If they do not draw spectators, they don't answer their purpose. The old method was most satisfactory to all parties; the publick was gratified by a procession; the criminal was supported by it. Why is all this to be swept away?'

Mandeville would have objected to this last argument that executions were supposed to support the criminal. He argued that only the fear of showing his own inward terror at such a moment and being taunted with cowardice enabled the criminal to suppress his fear of death. His guilt was public, his crimes proved; he was not dying for love of religion or country and it was unlikely that a poor rascal who could not read had so far lost himself 'in the Mazes of Philosophy, as to become a speculative Atheist'. Mandeville argued that from the moment of sentence the aim should be to break the criminal with a dark and solitary dungeon, a bread-and-water diet and the threat of dissection after death so that when seated in the cart the 'unspeakable Agonies of his excruciated Soul' would be visible by his restless posture, the wringing of his hands and the distortion of his features. In time this would bring about the desired effect and the Tyburn crowds would gradually dwindle and die away being sickened by such scenes. His suggestions were mild ones by the standards of the age. Others argued that hanging was not punishment enough and that its horrors should be intensified still more by added refinements such as branding, whipping, torture, breaking on the wheel, starving and flogging to death.

In 1783 the Tyburn executions came to an end. The long procession was abandoned and the executions were to be carried out in front of the debtors' door of Newgate, just where the street broadened in front of the Magpie and Stump. The change was instigated by the sheriffs whose main argument for change was the shocking behaviour of the crowd on such occasions. Instead of impressing on them the solemnity of the occasion, their behaviour was such that 'all the ends of public justice (are) defeated; all the effects of example, the terrors of death, the shame of punishment, are all lost' on the riotous gathering with its carnival atmosphere in which 'profane jokes, swearing and blasphemy' were pre-eminent. The dying speech tended to be ignored and the holiday atmosphere weakened any possibility of others being deterred from crime.

Although they were against the procession the sheriffs remained convinced that the executions should continue to be public and hoped that some solemnity could be restored to the occasion by better stage-management, such as draping the scaffold in black, the tolling of the prison bell and solemn procession of officials to accompany the prisoners onto the gallows. It was hoped that such effects would be beneficial to the prisoners in the gaol, who could hear the bell, and to the spectators.

The first execution was carried out at Newgate on 9th December 1783.

New drop

All kinds of levity, jeering, laughing, hooting, whistling, even at the moment
the man is coming up. While he is still suffering—while he is struggling,
and his body writhing there is all this noise going on—obscene
expressions—anything but the impression which people might imagine
would be caused by the spectacle.

Evidence of City Police Superintendent
Charles Hodgson to the Select Committee
Inquiry to Take into Consideration the
present Mode of carrying into effect
Capital Punishments (1856)

On 9th December 1783 the new drop was used for the first time outside
Newgate when Edward Dennis and his assistant hanged ten people at once.
Some would have strangled and some would have died of broken necks but
it was all a matter of chance. However, the laborious fitting up and dis-
mantling of the scaffold each time prompted the Newgate Committee to ask
George Dance if there was not some way that this could be improved upon.
In December 1786 he reported to the City Lands Committee that he had
closely looked at the workings of the last execution and found that twelve
men were employed in taking down the scaffold from half past ten o' clock
in the morning to nearly five o' clock in the afternoon, but that twenty men
had been needed to set it up the night before from ten o' clock in the evening
to seven the next morning. Two more men were supposed to have been
hired but they did not turn up. He understood from the contractor, Mr
Banner, that his workmen were very reluctant to undertake the work and
that several had left his employment rather than be involved in such a
business and as a result he had lost some very valuable workmen. Dance
didn't specify any figures, although he later quotes a figure of 6s 8d that was
paid to each man for one day and one night's work, but he assumed that they
must have been paid extra as the only refreshment they had throughout that
long night was a pint of beer each.

He itemizes the contractor's account as follows:

'Twenty men from ten o' clock on Tuesday night to seven the next
morning.
Twenty pints of porter. Thirty links. Twenty-four candles. One pound of
soap. One pint of oil.'

The following year Dance was ordered to design 'a proper Erection for
the purpose of executing criminals. . .' Apparently he did so, though
existing prints show little variation on the original scaffold except for the
twin cross-beams being replaced by a single beam. He continued to improve
on the existing designs and submitted one for a new triangular-shaped

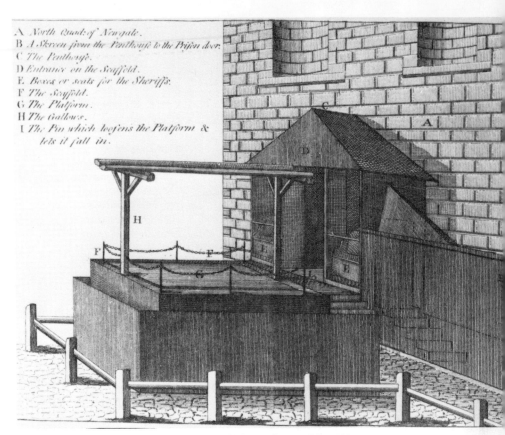

A North Quadr. of Newgate.
B A Screen from the Penthouse to the Prison door.
C The Penthouse.
D Entrance on the Scaffold.
E Boxes or seats for the Sheriffs.
F The Scaffold.
G The Platform.
H The Gallows.
I The Pin which loosens the Platform &
   lets it fall in.

The new drop outside Newgate which was first used in 1783.

gallows, presumably modelled on Tyburn, which could be swiftly erected by slotting each post into stone sockets permanently fixed in the ground. This was apparently constructed but again no print survives. There is a print of Thomas Rowlandson's dated 1806 which shows that the built-up scaffold has been done away with and that the gallows is a simple cross-beam on two supporting legs. The 1783 design had been a built-up platform with a drop which, presumably, in this period of experimentation, must have been done away with, and at some date in the Regency there was a reversion to the original design; the platform and drop were restored together with the covered-in walk from the prison and the porch and steps that led on to the scaffold.

Such accidents that did occur were not due to faults in the gallows' construction but, as before, with the behaviour of the executioners. Dennis' assistant was William Brunskill who, at his first execution, was so overcome with nervousness that after he had succesfully launched seven white-capped bodies through the trap, made a deep bow to the crowd as if asking for their applause. At the hanging of Clench and Mackley in June 1797 he hadn't secured the trap bolts and was still fixing the ropes, with the Ordinary and a

An execution at Newgate. By Thomas Rowlandson (1806).

priest beside him praying with the two men, when the trap gave way. Clench and Mackley died almost instantly (neither of them wearing the whitecap), while Brunskill and his assistant tumbled through the trap on top of the two clergymen, one of whom was badly hurt. The incident came to be regarded as some sort of omen as afterwards it was thought that the two men were innocent of the crime for which they were hanged.

One of the more barbarous punishments that survived the change to Newgate was the burning of women despite the fact, as in 1785, the new gallows could take up to twenty persons at once; on that occasion the prisoners had marched on to the scaffold, two by two, singing a funeral hymn. The usual one was the fifty-first psalm, which was irreverently known as 'The Hanging Song'. Burning was a punishment for women convicted of treason, murdering their husbands or instigating others to do so (Catherine Hayes came into this category) and coining offences; these were referred to as high or petty treason.

When a Member of Parliament tried to extend this barbaric penalty to make it treason to coin copper, Sir William Meredith rose to protest at one of the debates in 1777:

By this nick-name of treason, however, there lies at this moment in Newgate, under sentence to be burnt alive, a girl just turned 14; at her master's bidding she hid some white-washed farthings behind her stays, on which the jury found her guilty as an accomplice with her master in the treason. The master was hanged last Wednesday; and the faggots all lay ready, no reprieve came till just as the cart was setting out, and the girl would have been burnt alive on the same day, had it not been for the humane but casual interference of Lord Weymouth. Good God! Sir, we are taught to execrate the fires of Smithfield, and are we lighting them now to burn a poor harmless child for hiding a white-washed farthing?

According to Blackstone burning was the lesser punishment as 'the decency due to the sex forbids the exposing and publicly mangling' of bodies which treason proscribed and which for men meant partial hanging, stripping naked, castration, disembowelling and quartering. With burning, provided the hangman went about his work correctly, the woman might be strangled or at least unconscious before the flames touched her.

The last woman to be burned alive was Christian Murphy on 18th March 1789. She and her husband had been sentenced to death for coining offences. He was one of eight men brought from Newgate soon after eight o' clock and put on the scaffold. After praying and singing a psalm, which was popularly known as 'The Prisoner's Lamentation', possibly the fifty-first, the trap dropped. Once the hangman was satisfied that they were dead there was a pause of several minutes before Murphy was brought out and chained to a stake which was a few yards nearer to Newgate Street than the scaffold. She was wearing a white dress. The stake, in fact, was a small gibbet and after a few minutes spent in prayer she mounted a stool and was hung from the projecting arm. After she had hung for thirty minutes faggots were heaped over her head, so that she was completely covered, and burned. Among the spectators was Sir Benjamin Hammet, who was there in his official capacity as sheriff. The following May he introduced into Parliament a bill which would change the law and abolish such scenes for ever. Obviously the experience had greatly affected him for he said that, although a sheriff was open to prosecution if he did not carry out a sentence which had been ordered by a court, there was not a man in England who would carry it into effect. He described the law as a 'savage remnant of Norman policy'. The Act was passed that same session and judicial burnings came to an end.

Among the execution accounts of this time there are references to a particular piece of gallows superstition and that is the curative power of a dead man's hands. At a mass execution and burning in 1786 twelve spectators went up to the gallows, where the executioner rubbed the still warm hands of the six dangling bodies upon their necks and faces as a supposed cure for wens. The same thing happened again when William Hollings was hanged for murder. Three females were rubbed with the dead man's hands.

'The first was a young woman of interesting appearance who was so much affected by the ceremony, that she was obliged to be supported.' Wood shavings from the gallows were supposed to be a cure for the ague if carried in a bag round the neck. Headaches were supposed to be cured if a halter, with which anyone had been hanged, was tied about the head. (So they would!) One of the more bizarre examples was that of a highwayman who kept the bone fragments, after his jawbone had been shot away, and gave them away as good-luck tokens to his fellow-prisoners in Newgate shortly before he was hanged.

Cato Street conspirators

He had now to pronounce upon them the sentence of the law, which was—
    That you, and each of you, be taken from hence to the gaol from whence you came, and from thence that you be drawn upon a hurdle to a place of execution, and be there hanged by the neck until you be dead; and that afterwards your heads shall be severed from your bodies, and your bodies be divided into four quarters, to be disposed of as his majesty shall think fit.
    And may God of his infinite goodness have mercy upon your souls.
Trial of the Cato Street conspirators (1820)

In 1820 Newgate was the scene for what was probably the most dramatic execution of the nineteenth century. Since the ending of the long, drawn-out wars with Revolutionary and Napoleonic France, working-class revolt had been steadily simmering and was showing itself now in disturbances, machine-breaking and protests against growing industrialization and the destruction of the old ways of life. Government ministers were generally well insulated from the effects of their policies, but in 1820 a daring coup was organized to assassinate the entire British cabinet including the Prime Minister and the Duke of Wellington. Unknown to the plotters the Government had been kept well informed of the course of the plot by its spies. The plotters were arrested in a stable loft in Cato Street, only a few minutes walk from the old Tyburn gallows, and after a fight, some were captured and brought to trial at the Sessions House, Old Bailey. Some were sentenced to transportation, but five—Thistlewood, Ings, Brunt, Davidson and Tidd—were ordered for execution on 30th April 1820. All were to be hanged and beheaded which was the penalty for traitors. By early morning, on the day of execution, the Old Bailey was choked with crowds.

Shortly after a quarter to seven, five coffins were brought on to the scaffold, which had been liberally sprinkled with sawdust. Thistlewood's

Cato Street Conspiracy. Capture of the conspirators in Cato Street.

(he was the ringleader) was the first to be lifted out and placed by the drop. The third coffin was longer than the others and it was supposed that it was for Davidson, who was the tallest of them. Each of the coffins was given a bed of sawdust to stop blood from seeping through.

Lastly the block itself was brought on to the platform and placed at the head of Thistlewood's coffin. Instead of a flat top the edge had been angled so that it was sharp. Soon after, the prisoners came on to the scaffold following behind the Ordinary, who was reading the Burial Service for the Dead.

Ings, Thistlewood and Tidd sucked oranges as they walked behind him. The crowd cheered them as they took up their positions on the drop and lifted their heads for the hangman to make the final adjustment. White caps were pulled over their faces and the drop released.

Thistlewood died almost instantly. He struggled for a few minutes and soon turned slowly round on the rope. Tidd scarcely moved at all and

Davidson after three or four heaves became motionless. Brunt and Ings died in great agony. The hangman's assistant had to pull on their legs before their struggles ended.

After hanging for one hour, the trap was put up again and the bodies were put in sitting positions in their coffins. Thistlewood's head was laid back so that it rested on the edge of the block. The cap was removed and the noose. For the beheading, an unknown man had been hired; possibly he was a surgeon or someone with medical knowledge. When he stepped on to the scaffold he was seen to be wearing a black mask down to his mouth, over which a coloured handerchief was tied, and a hat low on his forehead. Instead of the axe that had been provided he was carrying a surgeon's amputation knife.

Wanted notice for Arthur Thistlewood the leader of the conspiracy.

Numb. 17560. [373]

The London Gazette
EXTRAORDINARY.

Publi§hed by Authority.

THURSDAY, FEBRUARY 24, 1820.

Whitehall, February 23, 1820.

WHEREAS Arthur Thistlewood stands charged with High Treason, and also with the Wilful Murder of Richard Smithers, a reward of ONE THOUSAND POUNDS is hereby offered to any person or persons who shall discover and apprehend, or cause to be discovered and apprehended the said Arthur Thistlewood, to be paid by the Lords Commissioners of His Majesty's Treasury, upon his being apprehended and lodged in any of His Majesty's Gaols. And all persons are hereby cautioned upon their Allegiance not to receive or harbour the said Arthur Thistlewood, as any person offending herein will be thereby guilty of High Treason. SIDMOUTH.

The above-named Arthur Thistlewood is about forty-eight years of age, five feet ten inches high, has a sallow complexion, long visage, dark hair (a little grey), dark hazle eyes and arched eyebrows, a wide mouth and a good set of teeth, has a scar under his right jaw, is slender made, and has the appearance of a military man, was born in Lincolnshire, and apprenticed to an Apothecary at Newark, usually wears a blue long coat and blue pantaloons, and has been a Lieutenant in the Militia.

May-day Garland. The fiddler is the government spy who betrayed them.
The masked man is the one who did the beheading.

Left: *The execution of the conspirators.*

When the crowd saw him lay the edge of the knife to Thistlewood's throat they broke out into a storm of shouting and whistling. For a moment the headsman was disconcerted but he quickly recovered his composure and set to work. Once the head was severed he handed it to the hangman's assistant who held it up to the crowd and bellowed: 'This is the head of Arthur Thistlewood, the traitor.'

Ings, Tidd and Davidson were beheaded in the same manner. There was more shouting when Brunt's head was dropped into the sawdust. As the last head was being shown to the crowd the unknown headsman walked swiftly from the scaffold.

It had been a quarter to eight when Thistlewood mounted the scaffold and it was seven minutes to nine when Brunt's head was put in his coffin.

Capital convictions

What effects are produced by such executions?—They merely come to see an execution of that kind as a spectacle; they go away again and waste their time; and many of the spectators commit crimes, as I have reason to suppose, before the night closes, after witnessing such a scene: nay, we had a boy brought in some time ago, who had only a few days before been out of Newgate; he was brought in for picking pockets under the gallows; and when I spoke to him upon the subject, and said, 'How could you do such a thing at such an awful moment?' he said, 'Sir, that was the best moment in the world, for everybody's eyes were up when the drop was falling'.

Evidence of Rev. H. S. Cotton to the Select Committee Inquiry on Prisons in the City of London and Borough of Southwark (1818)

The beginning of the nineteenth century saw a marked change in the implementation of capital statutes. While the legislature was increasing the severity of sentences, the courts were adopting a more relaxed attitude to sentencing and fewer people were being hanged after being capitally convicted. Between 1756 and 1765, there were 329 persons capitally convicted and, of these, 183 were executed, which is more than half of all those sentenced. Between 1795 and 1804 the ratio was approximately one out of six: 819 persons were capitally convicted out of which 132 were executed. Just how sharp the drop was can be seen by comparing the first and last three years.*

	Capitally convicted	Executed
1756-8	90	51
1802-4	244	23

From the last dates the number of executions begins to fall.

(*See Radzinowicz Vol. 1 pp. 158-9)

Giving evidence to the Commission on Capital Punishment in 1866 the Rev. J. Davis, who had been Ordinary for the past twenty years, handed the committee a list of seventy-five names of persons who had been sentenced to death from and including 1840 up to the present day. Twenty-four executions had been carried out at Newgate but he didn't know of the remainder how many had been carried out elsewhere. When asked how he had felt after witnessing his first execution he said he had been ill for three days but now it was merely unpleasant. The most recent execution had been the five pirates of the 'Flowery Land', but the numbers had taken away the horrible nature of the thing. The Committee asked: 'It was more like war?' 'And they were cowards', he said agreeing. The experience had not been so shocking as the execution of one man.

Police Superintendent Hodgson said much the same thing. Before joining the City police he had been a soldier in Spain and had witnessed two executions by garrotting. He told a Select Committee in 1856 that in the past seventeen years he had seen twenty executions; the first one had dwelt in his mind, he dreaded the experience, but he could attend them now with indifference.

Between 1825 and 1831 the national statistic of persons sentenced to death was 9,316, but those carried out were considerably fewer. Out of the 410 persons convicted of horse-stealing, sheep-stealing, cattle-stealing and stealing in a dwelling-house to the value of £5 only seventy were executed. Similar sorts of statistics can be quoted for other offences. Much of the credit can go to Robert Peel who, when he began his reform of the criminal law in the 1820s, said that he hoped to 'break up the sleep of centuries'.

In 1837, there were 438 persons capitally convicted. Only two years later there had been a dramatic drop to fifty-six.

Nineteen out of twenty persons who were capitally convicted did not think that they would hang. Dickens realized this on his visit when he wrote that among the twenty-five to thirty prisoners he saw who had been sentenced, and were waiting for it to be confirmed, 'there was very little anxiety or mental suffering depicted' in their countenances, but he questioned 'whether there was a man among them, notwithstanding, who did not *know* that although he had undergone the ceremony, it was never intended that his life should be sacrificed'.

It was different with the two men he saw in the press room whom the turnkey told him were 'dead men'. One was stooped over the fire, his head sunk upon his arm, while the other was leaning on a window sill, the light falling on his pale, haggard face and wildly staring eyes.

Whether the Ordinary could offer much comfort is doubtful. The chapel itself had a sombre and gloomy air. From Dickens' description it was even more depressing: 'the bare and scanty pulpit, with the paltry painted pillars on either side—the women's gallery with its great heavy curtain—the men's with its unpainted benches and dingy front—the tottering little table at the

This is a 'fake' composition of the execution of the banker Henry Fauntleroy. Although the details are probably correct Fauntleroy, who is having his arms pinioned, was hanged alone and not with two others as the picture suggests.

altar, with the commandments on the wall above it, scarcely legible through lack of paint, and dust and damp . . .' and below the reading desk the 'huge black pen' which was the Condemned pew. The Condemned sermon guaranteed the Ordinary an audience and sometimes he abused the privilege. Of nobody was this probably more true than the Rev Horace Cotton, who was mocked by prisoners and prison staff alike. He was in a scourging mood, and had been for some Sundays past, when Henry Fauntleroy, a banker, was ordered to be executed for forgery. The week before Cotton had shattered the nerves of an eighteen-year old boy, hanged the next day, who had been present when a drunken Irishman was mugged of five shillings, and two weeks before that Cotton had sent a woman convicted of theft into hysterics. Now it was Fauntleroy's turn and by the time Cotton had finished the banker was so distressed that he had to be helped from the chapel. Afterwards Cotton was severely censured for harrowing the prisoner's feelings so unnecessarily.

In such circumstances it must have been most unpleasant to have to face the Ordinary in full canonicals next morning when the time came for irons to be struck off and the arms pinioned in the Press Room. At Governor Wall's execution in 1802 the Rev Brownlow Ford ordered the hangman to slacken off the cords (which were too tight, possibly because the hangman had not been paid his fee), and explained the mechanism of the gallows to the condemned man who had asked: 'Sir, I am informed that I shall go down with great force. Is that so?' They then said a few short prayers before setting off across the Press Yard.

Gallows, noose and St Sepulchre's bell

Ah! Calcraft came from a family of slow worms. He choked his prisoners to death. . . . . . He THROTTLED them, but I EXECUTE them.
William Marwood, Executioner, 1874-1883

It is doubtful whether anyone had ever considered the consequences of moving the gallows from Tyburn to Newgate, from a large open space to a restricted street in front of the prison. Outside the debtors' door, where the gallows was placed, the street was funnel-shaped, with the broad end facing St Sepulchre's church and the tapering spout towards Ludgate Hill. At this end of the street the crowd had very little room in which to manoeuvre.

In 1807 Haggerty and Holloway were ordered for execution for the murder of a lavender-maker five years before; although they protested their innocence they were convicted on the evidence of an informer. An enormous crowd, estimated at 40,000, gathered to see them hanged. The pressure was so great that people began to panic; some screamed, others shouted and a stampede started. Those that fell never got up again. The worst incident was at Green Arbour Lane, which is a courtyard in the broadest part of the Old Bailey. A couple of piemen were selling pies from a basket which they balanced on a stool. This was knocked over as the panic started. As one of the piemen stooped to pick up his scattered pies so people stumbled against him and fell over, setting up a chain-reaction which

An execution outside Newgate (1809). The City Marshal, who supervised the executions, is on horseback.

brought other people down. One woman just had time to hand her baby to a man before she overbalanced and was crushed to death; the baby was thrown over the heads of the crowd, from hand to hand, before being safely placed in a cart. Another cart sent some of its passengers spilling to the ground and some of those were among the final death toll. It was almost an hour before the streets could be cleared; the final total was twenty-eight dead and nearly seventy injured.

It was probably as a result of this accident that, when there was to be an execution, barricades or pens were erected in the surrounding streets from which the execution could be seen. But according to Inspector Kittle, giving evidence in 1866 to a Select Committee, there was no control over numbers, and the consequence was that they were so tightly wedged together that the spectators could not have extricated themselves even if they had wished to do so. He had often seen boys and lads passed over the heads of the crowd for a considerable distance.

The police protecting the scaffold stood inside a barrier placed about it. It had been pulled out by one or two horses (it was on wheels) and the finishing touches added during the night. All this time they would have been watched by the crowds, hundreds of whom slept on the steps of the prison or in St Sepulchre's churchyard. At 8 o'clock the prisoners' procession—the sheriffs in their robes and chains of office and the Ordinary in full canonicals and with a nosegay—emerged from the prison and stopped at the foot of the scaffold about two or three minutes before the man was to hang. Sheriff Nissen (1863/4) thought that St Sepulchre's church bell was no longer tolled at the time of execution but that the prison bell continued to be rung. From there the only persons that went forward were the prisoners, warders, the hangman and Ordinary. On average only sixteen days had elapsed since conviction. The crowd began its shout of 'Hats off' not as any mark of respect but to get a better view; if they were not taken off they were knocked off and thrown about, and the further they went away the louder was the applause. There was a lot of hooting, which one witness thought was more for the hangman than the prisoner.

When Greenacre stepped on to the gallows in 1837 he was so shaken that his last words were 'Don't leave me long with that pack of ghouls'. The practice of the prisoner making a last speech seems to have to died out in the 1840s though there is no precise date for this. Inspector Adam Spary told the Select Committee in 1856 that he had seen sixteen executions in the past eighteen years and he remembered some years before a criminal addressing the crowd but he couldn't recall its effect.

The hangman from 1829 to 1874 was William Calcraft. He would come onto the scaffold 'a dirty wide-awake hat on and a shooting jacket'; his explanation was 'I must keep my client in good spirits. Besides I am not a parson or an undertaker, and therefore decline to don funeral garments.' Sometimes he sported a large buttonhole; he was a keen amateur gardener and breeder of prize rabbits. As hangman he was one of the most—if not the most—incompetent. It was said of him that he would hang a man as he would hang a dog. He used a short drop of not more than two or three feet; this could mean the prisoners struggling for many minutes before losing consciousness. He would go into the pit and climb on their backs or pull their legs. It was possibly for this reason that by 1866 curtains had been fitted around the scaffold railings so that it was only the people in the windows opposite who could see what happened once the trap had fallen.

After the body had hung for one hour Calcraft would come on to the scaffold once more, take out a large pocket knife and cut the rope; the body would then drop through to the ground.

His use of the short drop led to awful scenes at the hanging of William Bousfield in March 1856. Peace had just been concluded and to celebrate the ending of the Crimean War all the City church bells were ringing in joyous celebration as Bousfield was carried on to the scaffold. He had already tried to commit suicide by flinging himself face down on a burning fire in his cell, but the warder with him had pulled him away and he had succeeded only in burning his mouth and the lower part of his face. Since being pinioned he had vomited so much that he was thought too weak to stand. He was carried on to the scaffold on a chair and was still sitting down as the trap fell away with its customary boom. The chair fell through but Bousfield didn't. Because of the short drop he was able to get both feet back on the platform and with a desperate effort was trying to raise his hands to the rope. One of the warders rushed forward and pushed his feet away but with a desperate effort the hooded man managed to swing himself to the other side of the drop and get his feet on to the edge. The crowd by this time were roaring and shrieking abuse. Calcraft, who had already left the scaffold, thinking it was all over once he had released the trap, was hurriedly called back and with a struggle forced Bousfield over the drop. To everyone's horror the desperate man managed to swing himself back yet a third time and struggled still to lift his hands up to the rope that was strangling him. Calcraft, with the help of two or three warders, forced him back over the drop yet again and held his legs steady until he died.

As Marwood would say 'Old Calcraft . . . *throttled* them, but I *execute* them'.

When Mayhew and Binney visited Newgate as part of their research for their monumental work on the London prisons, which they published in 1862, they were taken to the ante-room of the keeper's office where they were shown three rows of plaster busts of murderers who had been hanged at Newgate. These were taken after death and on nearly all of them the rope marks could be seen where they had buried deep into the flesh. The deputy keeper, who showed them around, told them that he had seen twenty-nine criminals hanged in front of Newgate. When Greenacre had been hanged the houses fronting on to Newgate had charged spectators three guineas a time for viewing, and at some of the other houses the spectators had been charged two sovereigns for a seat on the roof! One anecdote he told them was of Mary Ann Hunt, who had been convicted of murder in 1847; when asked by the Clerk of Arraigns if there was any reason why sentence of death should not be passed on her she replied that she was pregnant. A jury of

Execution of the 'Flowery Land' pirates (1864).

Birdcage Walk, the prison graveyard. Ninety-seven people were buried here and only their initials were carved on the walls. On the left can clearly be seen the initials of the Cato Street Conspirators — Thistlewood, Brunt, Ings, Davidson and Tidd.

twelve women was sworn to examine her. After they had been absent from the court for some time they returned and stated that she was not pregnant. Fortunately she was again examined by the prison doctor and found to be eight months gone!

The deputy governor had seen only two women executed. He complacently added 'The murderers generally sleep well on the night before their execution'. After sentence had been carried out the coffin was brought into one of the wards and the body buried the same afternoon in the presence of the governor or the under-sheriffs.

The burial yard was a long passage about eight feet wide; on one side was the female wing and on the other the high exterior wall of the prison which backed on to the old meat market. The passage had an overhead grating, through which the sky could be seen, and it was referred to for these reasons as Birdcage Walk. Prisoners had to walk along this passage from the prison to the court and in doing so knew what they were walking over because of the uneven paving stones which gradually tilted as the bodies mouldered away in their shrouds. Along the walls the murderers' initials were cut above where they were lying. One was marked 'B L D L W' and beneath it the words 'Ship Flowery Land Feb 1864'; these were five seamen who had been hanged for piracy. Further on were the initials of the Cato Street conspirators—T B I D T.

Mayhew and Binney concluded: 'This plain-looking passage is invested with tragic interest, when we think of the mouldering bones of the murderers rotting beneath, and carry our imagination back to the deeds of horror they transacted, the recital of which has brought paleness to many a cheek.'

'Hats off'

It is not right, perhaps, that a murderer's death should be surrounded by all the pious and tender accessories which accompany the departure of a good man to a better world, but most assuredly the sight of public executions to those who have to witness them is as disgusting as it must be demoralising even to all the hordes of thieves and prostitutes it draws together. Yesterday the assembly was of its kind an orderly one, yet it was such as we feel grateful to think will under the new law never be drawn together again in England.

The Times, 27th May 1868

Contrary to public opinion, Charles Dickens was not a frequent spectator of executions; in fact, he probably did not witness more than three or four in his lifetime and one of those would have been in Italy. In 1840 he sat up all night to watch the execution of Courvoisier outside Newgate. He was appalled by what he saw and ever afterwards would speak of the experience with the greatest of horror. He came away from it feeling, as did his companions, that despite the awfulness of the crime he would have rescued the murderer had it been possible. Six years later came his famous letters to *The Times*, one of them being sent on the day that the Mannings, husband and wife, were hanged at Horsemonger Lane Gaol. Gradually, in time, Dickens moved away from his abolitionist attitudes and at the end of his life was most decidedly in favour of hanging, as were many of his contemporaries. But, like Fielding, he believed that such hangings should be in private and that the streets should be freed of the loathsome scenes that attended such executions.

Parliament was steadily moving in the same direction. In 1866 the Report of the Capital Punishment Commission recommended that an Act should be passed putting an end to public executions; with few exceptions all the witnesses had been in favour.

The following year the Capital Punishment Within Prison Bill came before the House. The main proposal was that public hangings should be done away with. By now most people accepted that they were not a deterrent to crime. The lawlessness and brutality that accompanied such spectacles it was felt should be done away with and that the hangings should take place in private behind the prison walls. Those who wanted capital punishment abolished altogether were against such a proposal as, so they argued, in this way hanging would be allowed to continue. With hindsight, there is a lot of support for one of their other arguments that private executions such as this would enable the hangman to continue his bunglings, and well into the twentieth century the official statements frequently glossed over the fact that death had probably not been instantaneous. It was amidst these controversies that the Bill became law in May 1868.

Safeguards were written into the Capital Punishment Amendment Act that those to be hanged should suffer no unusual punishment; that a surgeon had to examine the body immediately after execution and that a death certificate should be signed by the sheriff, gaoler and prison chaplain. A coroner's inquest had to follow within twenty-four hours and the body itself was to be buried within the walls of the prison where the hanging had taken place.

It was while the Bill was passing through Parliament that Michael Barrett became the last man to be publicly hanged in Britain. He had been convicted for his part in the attempted rescue of fellow Fenians in Clerkenwell by exploding a hole in the wall of the prison and in doing so had killed four persons, two of them children, and injuring forty or so others.

His execution date was 26th May 1868. There were the usual scenes the night before the execution, such as 'cat-calls, comic choruses, dances, and even mock hymns', which continued until about 2 a.m. when the public houses closed. The crowd was an orderly one with many young women and children present. Crush barriers had been put up all about the scaffold and these were lined with velvet hats and huge white feathers. 'It is said that one sees on the road to the Derby such animals as are never seen elsewhere; so on execution morning; one sees faces that are never seen save round the gallows or near a great fire.'

As the bells began to toll there was the usual shout of 'Hats off' and screams and struggles from those in front as the crowd involuntarily pushed forward. Barrett was still wearing the claret-coloured coat and grey trousers that he had worn during his trial. His face was white as marble but he walked up coolly and calmly to the beam accompanied by a priest. The roars died down to a silence as Calcraft slipped the cap over his face and adjusted the rope about his neck. Barrett turned, and speaking through the hood, asked for the rope to be altered which the hangman did. From the moment the drop fell Barrett never moved.

When the hour was up for the body to be cut down the immense crowd that still waited began to shout: 'Come on, body snatcher! Take away the man you've killed.'

'The hangman appeared and cut down the body amid such a storm of yells and execrations as has seldom been heard even from such a crowd.'

The Fatal tree

London yesterday witnessed the last of those hideous spectacles familiar enough to the hard eyes of our predecessors, but more and more repulsive to the taste of these days.

The Times, 27th May 1868

The Clerkenwell explosion and its attempted rescue of prisoners so alarmed the Corporation that the very next day, 14th December 1867, the Gaol Committee ordered the City Police Commissioner, Colonel James Fraser, with the City Architect, to inspect Newgate and suggest ways of tightening security. At the same time he was ordered to provide three extra constables for the court so that one would always be on duty, night or day. Fraser had been a professional soldier before becoming Commissioner and the hand-written report, dated 25th December 1867, delegated to a Royal Engineers Captain, offered a military solution which was strongly reminiscent of sieges and fortifications. Echoes of the Gordon Riots linger in the report and there is a feeling throughout that the Captain was thinking of repelling a mob or an army rather than of thwarting a gaol-break by a handful of desperate men.

On the three sides facing the Sessions House Yard, the Old Bailey and Newgate Street the prison was comparatively secure against a surprise attack. Certain small improvements could be made, such as extra guards at the entrance to the keeper's house, an extra door between the prison vestibule and the keeper's quarters and a strong door between the pinioning room and the main prison. However, these faded into insignificance compared with what was found on the fourth side facing Warwick Square at the back of the prison. In the Captain's own words: 'the state of things struck me as very remarkable; houses occupied by private parties are built along the entire length of the exterior of the prison wall, in some instances the upper parts of these houses having even been *erected on the top of the prison wall* with windows looking into the prison passage leading from the Sessions House to the prison . . . the fact of these houses being on the position described would admit of prisoners when at exercise being rescued by a body of determined friends (who for the occasion need neither be numerous nor particularly ingenious), before assistance could be obtained from the other parts of the prison.'

In other words the windows were directly above Birdcage Walk with a clear view of the comings and goings along the passage. The Captain continued that from those houses it would be difficult to set fire to the prison but quite easy to blow it up! Even the posting of extra sentries was of questionable value as they could easily be dispatched from the prison wall and possibly before they could raise any alarm. In his opinion the first step in any improvements was to pull down the entire row of houses abutting on to the prison wall. Next a wall, some twenty-four feet high, should be built and at its base a slight ditch with a slope which would stop gunpowder barrels from being rolled against it.

With this last suggestion, and the others to follow, the officer was quite unconsciously recommending a return to the original Roman fortifications even to the extent of constructing a defensive ditch.

The wall would have loopholes for rifles and there should be an overhang of about six feet, perhaps of iron, so that the guards could sweep the outer wall with rifle fire. The Sessions House Yard should have a similar wall but no ditch. The wall facing Newgate Street should have in addition a form of barbican thrown out from the upper part of the wall for flanking that side; while the two prison entrances in Old Bailey should be protected by projecting galleries through which missiles could be dropped on attackers and flanking fire could be raked along the outer face of the prison and directed at the entrance to the keeper's house; the latter, as at the time of the Gordon Riots, was the weakest point on that side. His final suggestion was that Birdcage Walk should have its iron grating replaced by a solid one and the flanking wall have loopholes so that the top of it could be inspected in case of explosive charges being laid there.

Had his plans been carried out it would have turned Newgate into a fortress and, to recapitulate, such proposals might have been acceptable if the imagined danger had been on the scale of the Gordon riots. They were, however, an over-reaction, and financially impracticable as a security measure against a possible gaol-break.

The crisis over Newgate began its slow slide to oblivion. As from 31st December 1881 it ceased to exist as a prison and became just a temporary place of detention for prisoners on trial or awaiting execution. After Barrett's hanging the gallows was re-erected in a shed in one of the exercise yards; it was not the beam from the Newgate scaffold but came from

Horsemonger Lane gaol and was reckoned by a later hangman as being the finest in the country as it could take three persons at once. The shed was overlooked by a depressing attic which was known as the Hangman's Room where the hangman slept the night before an execution. The room was pitted with the hangmen's names which had been carved in the woodwork.

The last execution carried out at Newgate was shortly before the prison's closing on Tuesday 6th May 1902. The murderer was twenty-one-old George Woolfe, who had kicked and stabbed his girl friend seventeen times with a piece of broken file before dumping her body in a ditch on Tottenham Marshes. The trial had been brief. Woolfe had told friends that he intended to get 'shunt' of her. After the killing he enlisted in the army under a false name, but was given away by his father and convicted despite his denials.

He was hanged at eight o' clock in the morning. As laid down in the new regulations, there had been three Sundays between sentence and execution; a black flag fluttered over the prison and the prison bell with its 'curious note which rolled all over the prison and seemed to breathe the very spirit of pain and terror' tolled for the last time.

In a matter of months Newgate was a place for the souvenir hunters. A large crowd of bidders followed the auctioneer through the long dreary corridors on a bleak February day. Among the buyers was John Tussaud, buying on behalf of Madame Tussaud's Waxworks. 'I see that procession now, some muffled to the ears, some blowing their finger-tips in the piercing cold, others stamping their feet, but all indulging in one form of humour or another to keep up their spirits in very dispiriting surroundings.'

Nine death masks were sold for five guineas. A set of original leg chains and weights which had been found in the dungeons went for £4 10s. Mrs Fry's door from the exercise yard to the debtors' prison fetched £20. Chubb's bought the outer door of solid iron, which had opened on to the scaffold, for £9 10s. According to his own account John Tussaud bought Jack Sheppard's cell, which was clearly impossible. What he did purchase was a door for £3 10s. and a wrought iron grill for £1 17s. 6d. both of which came from the chapel staircase to the roof; these were in addition to some cells, which were marked as they were taken down and rebuilt at Tussaud's, one of them as Sheppard's cell.

The highlight of the sale was the prison bell, which went to Tussaud for £100 amidst a round of applause from the spectators. One reason for its high price was that it was thought to contain, but didn't, a high quantity of silver. For the first time in 150 years the couplet on it could be read:

Ye people all who hear me ring,
Be faithful to your God and King.

Below it was the maker's name, Pack and Chapman of London, Fecit 1775.

The fittings of Newgate Prison were brought to the hammer on February 4 and realised a little short of £1,000. Madame Tussaud's paid £100 for the old tolling bell. Elizabeth Fry's door was bought by Mr. Barclay as a family heirloom for £20. The entrance door from Newgate Street was bought by the Chubbs (for its old Bramah lock) for £30. A warder's key cupboard fetched £12 10s. The condemned prisoners' pew fetched £3 5s.

MEMORIES OF JACK SHEPPARD   AND ELIZABETH FRY

The Death Bell

Spyhole and Food Grating in a Cell Door

Fine Old Cast-iron Cistern

The Execution Shed   The Auction last Week   Condemned Prisoners' Chapel Seat

Old Oak and Iron Door   Another Old Oak Door   A Historic Door
Known as Elizabeth Fry's door   Which led from the staircase to the women's gallery and chapel   Through which Jack Sheppard escaped

The remnants of Newgate prison brought to the hammer.

Tyburn nuns

Only a week or two after the auction, mass was said for the first time at the Tyburn convent at 6 Hyde Park Place, just a few hundred yards west of the site of the Tyburn tree. To Roman Catholics the triple tree was and is something more then 'the nubbing cheat' or the 'three-legged mare'; it was a place of martyrdom where 106 martyrs had died for their faith between 1535 and 1681. Many of the martyrs had been sustained through their terrible ordeal of hanging and mutilation, not only by their faith but by the behaviour of their followers, who had risked imprisonment and worse by sometimes decorating the triple tree with sweet-smelling herbs, flowers, branches of bay and laurel and by asking for their blessing even at the gallows' foot. After execution their followers had risked their lives by rescuing the martyrs' bodies or some relic from the pit into which the mangled remains had been flung after execution.

As a result of the Law of Association which was passed by the French Government in July 1901 many religious communities went into exile rather than be dissolved. Among them was the order of the Adorers of the Sacred Heart of Jesus of Montmartre, who were welcomed by the English Catholic community. It was thought appropriate that nuns 'from the French Mount of Martyrs should take root on the English Mount of Martyrs', the latter a glowing euphemism for Tyburn hill. The present house was bought and Mass said for the first time on 6th March 1903 in the new shrine of the Tyburn Martyrs.

In the basement chapel there are chilling reminders of Tyburn's dreadful past. Mounted on the walls are fragments of bone and cloth and prints of savage executions; each of the nuns is named after a English martyr although not always after one that was executed at Tyburn.

The most dramatic thing of all is the altar which is straddled by a free-standing construction of the triple tree itself, smaller than the original, but with altar lamps, not bodies, hanging from each beam.

Birdcage Walk

Among the first things to be cleared out from the prison were the bodies in Birdcage Walk. Because it was unconsecrated ground it was not subject to the usual rules, and the ground had been dug over many times with skulls and bones always being turned up but reburied near to the spot where they had first laid. None of them could be identified. The ground was dug out

The triple tree altar at the Tyburn convent. The height of the original would have been half as high again.

and the remains of ninety-two bodies removed and reburied at the City of London cemetery at Ilford. The oldest bodies had been put there in 1820, but according to the Medical Officer of Health these would probably have disintegrated. According to a plan ninety-seven people were buried in the passage; the missing five bodies may have belonged to the Cato Street conspirators, who were the oldest burials, and presumably those to which the Medical Officer was referring.

When the auction took place people were seen digging in the passage in the hope of finding bones or teeth. None was apparently found.

By then the gallows had been taken down, not for destruction such as had happened at Tyburn, but to Pentonville prison where it was used for the first time on 30th September 1902, only four short months after it had been used for the last execution in Newgate.

Conclusion

Ye hangmen of Old England,
How sturdily you stood,
A-smoking pipes by Tyburn Tree,
A-swigging pots in the Old Bailee,
And strung up all you could.
Old Ballad

When work was begun on demolishing the gaol in 1902, cells of corrugated iron and plaster were erected in the old Press Yard capable of housing eighty-one prisoners to keep the Sessions going. The new Central Criminal Court followed the lines of the old prison and on the Old Bailey side was faced with as much of the original prison stone as practicable. The building took five years to finish and was capped with a bronze figure of Justice with her scales and upraised sword. Contrary to popular belief the figure is not blindfolded. She can see which way the scales will dip and where to strike. Her impact on the underworld was less imposing. One cynical prisoner said sourly: 'Justice was so perishing high up that he couldn't see it!' Above the main door is the massive stone figure of the Recording Angel and on either side of her Fortitude and Truth; below them is the prayer book version of a verse from psalm 72:

Defend the Children of the Poor: Punish the Wrong-doer.

The focal point of the new building was Number 1 Court, where most of the great murder trials of this century have taken place. The oak panelling, the dock, the warders, the prisoner and facing them the scarlet judge, the Sword of Justice behind him and the silk death cap, gave a shape, colour and drama to the trials which the old courts had never had. And so the mystique of the Old Bailey, its popular name, was born.

An added dimension when the courts reopened was the giving of evidence by the defendants themselves. For centuries they had depended on the advocacy of counsel to secure an acquittal but now, because of a change of law in 1898, they could be heard to speak, be something more than a silent spectator to their lives, a little more than a breathing wax effigy. Crippen, Seddon, Heath, the Shepherd's Bush killers, the Krays, Christie, the Houndsditch Murderers were just a part of the roll-call of English murder which gave the Central Criminal Court as a whole its own peculiar mystique and global reputation.

It was William Roughead who gave this mystique its expression:

Murder has a magic of its own, its peculiar alchemy. Touched by that crimson wand, things base and sordid, things ugly and of ill report, are transformed into matters wondrous, weird and tragical. Dull streets become fraught with mystery, commonplace dwellings assume a sinister aspect,

everyone concerned, howsoever plain and ordinary, is invested with a new
value and importance as the red light falls upon each. The moveless figure in
the dock, the passing cloud of witnesses, even the poor and pitiful exhibits,
all are endowed with a different character and hold for a space the popular
attention ere they revert once again to their customary and homely selves.

Old Bailey bombings

We went down and down, I never realised you could go down so far at the
Old Bailey. I thought we were going to hell.

> *Gang leader Charles Richardson after being*
> *sentenced to twenty-five years imprisonment for his part in the*
> *so-called 'Torture Trial' (1967)*

Inevitably the Old Bailey has become a target for extremists of all sorts, for
defacing, destroying and demonstrating. It has twice been bombed, once in
the Blitz and once in an IRA bombing campaign in 1973.

May 10th 1941 was the night when London was to be 'Coventrated'. By
the time the German bombers headed for home London was a sea of flames
with more than 2,000 fires raging, nearly 1,500 dead and a score of land-
marks hit, such as the Tower, Westminster Abbey, the Houses of Parliament and the Old Bailey itself.

This was the third time that the Court had been hit, and high explosives
had devastated the Newgate Street end of the building. Number Two Court
had been wrecked and three others littered with debris. Marble slabs had
been wrenched away from the walls; some of the frescoes had been
destroyed and figures below the dome had been cracked. In places the roof
had gone with the public rooms and Number Two Court was open to the
sky. Fortunately there were no casualties. On an earlier raid two of the
porters had been killed when inspecting the upper storeys. The traditional
ceremony of opening the Sessions continued as usual but this time in one of
the dining-rooms which was converted into a temporary court.

On Thursday 8th March 1973 a car bomb was exploded outside the Court
as part of a Provisional IRA bombing campaign on London which was
designed to bring the capital to its knees. The main targets that day were
Scotland Yard and the Old Bailey, both symbols of law and order. Because
of a one-day railway strike the usual parking restrictions had been lifted and

The Central Criminal Court after it had been damaged by bombing on 10 May 1941.

the bombers were able to park their car directly outside the Court. On detonating, the bomb disintegrated the car completely, parts of it being found on the roof, which was seventy-five feet above street level. Most of the injuries to the 200 casualities were caused by flying glass; the front of a nearby sixteen-storey building disintegrated completely. Miraculously nobody was killed though two police officers who were close to the explosion point, one of them only twenty feet away, were badly injured, one nearly losing his leg and the other almost his arm. Because of an early warning the nineteen courts had been evacuated, except for a murder trial which adjourned to one of the jury rooms for the judge to give a short summing up, and the police were clearing the streets when the car bomb exploded. One of the peculiar effects of the blast was that some of the glass doors nearest to the explosion were undamaged, while those at Court 16, the furthest away, were wrenched from the walls and shattered to fragments. Above one of the main staircases fragments of window glass had been driven deep into the concrete, where one of them still remains as a grim reminder of 'Bloody Thursday'.

With the demolition of the gaol and the passing of the 'fetid and corrupt atmosphere' that was the 'heynhouse gaol of Newgate' it might have seemed that the site had been exorcised forever. If any ghosts still linger they must have chuckled when a twelve-year-old girl, the youngest defendant to have appeared at the Central Criminal Court this century, was stood in the dock with her mother and fifteen-year-old brother to answer charges of shoplifting. Her head was barely visible above the dock; she was charged with stealing an iced bun and a doughnut from a supermarket.

The date, astonishingly, was July 1981!

The IRA bombing on 8 March 1973.

By one of those quirks of legal procedure the case had found its way to the Central Criminal Court where it is common in the summer months, because it has twenty-three courts, to help clear some of the backlog that has built up in the provincial courts. This particular case had been transferred from a court which had a backlog of 1,900 cases.

After a brief consultation with counsel the judge ordered both children's immediate release and the charges to be dropped.

In the resulting furore, newspapers pointed out that it was at the Old Bailey in 1835 that a ten-year-old was transported for life for theft and that three boys aged twelve, thirteen and fourteen had been sentenced to death for burglary.

Newgate Cant

As black as Newgate's knocker: as black as the knocker on the prison door.

Cant: the language of the underworld; *Sadler's Memoirs,* anon. (1677): 'In the college of *Newgate* he learnt to Cant by Rote'.

Go west: 'Let them go Westward to the Triple Tree . . .', John Taylor, the water poet.

In the Newgate: in the inside pocket where the pickpockets cannot reach.

Lord of the Manor of Tyburn: the common hangman.

Newgate: in Roman times the main gate to the west.
Newgate bird: a thief that was frequently caged in Newgate.
Newgate Calendar: biographies of criminals, generally written by the Ordinary of Newgate, published as pamphlets or broadsides, and later brought together in book form beginning in 1773.
Newgate collar, frill or fringe: the collar of the beard below the chin where the hangman's rope would sit.
Newgate fashion: two by two, which is how the prisoners were marched when they were taken to a ship for transportation.
Newgate frisk or hornpipe: dancing in the air, a hanging.
Newgate knocker: the shape of the lock of hair which thieves sometimes twisted back towards the ear and which was supposed to resemble Newgate's knocker.
Newgate nightingale: an early synonym of Newgate gaol-bird.
Newgate prison: sited at the corner of Newgate Street and Old Bailey. From medieval times it was the gatehouse itself with extensions to the north and south. It was rebuilt several times. The last rebuilding was 1770 to 1783, by George Dance the younger. Demolished in 1902.
Newgate ring: a moustache and beard combined, with the side-whiskers clean shaven.
Newgate seize me!:   among criminals a solemn and binding oath.
Newgate solicitor: a rogue lawyer who helped criminals to escape justice.

Old Bailey: a street running south from Newgate Street to Ludgate Hill. Originally Le Bayl (1290), le Bayly (1305/6), The Bailey without Newgate (1307), le Baille without Ludegate (1311), Olde bailly (1481).
Old Bailey underwriter: a small-time forger.

Rumboe: Newgate prison (eighteenth-century slang).

To take a ride to Tyburn: to go to your own hanging.
Tyburn: a former tributary of the Thames rising at Hampstead; a principal place of execution from 1177 to 1783 (a plaque at the junction of present day Oxford Street and Edgware Road marks the spot).
Tyburn blossom: 'a young thief or pick-pocket, who will in time ripen into fruit borne by the deadly never-green'.
Tyburn collar: see Newgate collar.

Tyburn ticket: a certificate granted under a statute of William III to persons who had succesfully prosecuted a criminal on a capital conviction and which exempted them from all parish and ward offices within the parish or ward in which the felony had been committed. This, and the privileges which the certificate conferred, could be sold once only. The Act was repealed in 1818.

Tyburn tippet: the hangman's halter.

Tyburn tree: the popular name for the gallows which was triangular in shape; that is why it was also known as the three-legged mare. As many as eight people could hang from each beam at once, twenty-four at a time. Taken down in 1759 but executions continued at Tyburn to 1783.

Up the hill: to ride in the condemned carts, from Newgate to Tyburn, by way of Holborn Hill, which is now modern day Holborn.

Whittington's Palace or The Whit: nicknames for Newgate after it was rebuilt by the executors of Richard Whittington, three times Mayor of London.

Select Bibliography

BABINGTON, ANTHONY: *The English Bastille* (Macdonald, 1971).

BASSETT, MARGERY: 'Newgate Prison in the Middle Ages', (*Speculum* Vol. 18, 1943).

BELL, WALTER G: *The Great Plague in London 1665* (Bodley Head, rev. ed., 1951); *The Great Fire of London 1666* (Bodley Head, rev. ed. 1951).

BELLAMY, JOHN: *Crime and Public Order in England in the later Middle Ages* (Routledge and Kegan Paul, 1973).

BERNARDI, JOHN: *A short history of the life of Major John Bernardi* (published London, by the author, 1729).

BLEACKLEY, HORACE: *The Hangmen of England* (Chapman and Hall, 1929).

BLEACKLEY, HORACE, and ELLIS, S. M.: *Trial of Jack Sheppard* (William Hodge, 1933).

COCKBURN, J. S. (Ed.): *Crime in England, 1550-1800* (Methuen, 1977).

COLLINS, PHILIP: *Dickens and Crime* (Macmillan, 2nd ed., 1965).

COOPER, DAVID D.: *The Lesson of the Scaffold* (Allen Lane, 1974).

DEFOE, DANIEL: *The History of the Press Yard* (London, T. Moor, 1717).

DOBB, C.: 'Henry Goodcole, Visitor of Newgate, 1620-1641'. (The Guildhall Miscellany No. 4, February 1955).

DORAN, DR: *London in the Jacobite Times* (Richard Bentley, 1877).

DUDDEN, F. HOMES: *Henry Fielding, His Life, Works, and Times* (Clarendon Press, 1952).

EARLE, PETER: *Monmouth's Rebels* (Weidenfeld and Nicolson, 1977).

GORDON, CHARLES: *The Old Bailey and Newgate* (T. Fisher Unwin, 1902).

GRIFFITHS, ARTHUR: *Chronicles of Newgate* (Chapman and Hall, 1884).

HAY, LINEBAUGH, RULE, THOMPSON and WINSLOW: *Albion's Fatal Tree* (Penguin, 1977).

HIBBERT, CHRISTOPHER: *The Roots of Evil* (Weidenfeld and Nicolson, 1963).

HOLLINGSWORTH, KEITH: *The Newgate Novel, 1830-1847* (Wayne State University Press, 1963).

HOOPER, W. EDEN: *History of Newgate and the Old Bailey* (Underwood Press, 1935).

HOPKINS, R. THURSTON: *Life and Death at the Old Bailey* (Herbert Jenkins, 1935).

HOWARD, JOHN: *The State of the Prisons in England and Wales* (Warrington, printed by Eyres, 1780).

HOWSON, GERALD: *Thief-taker General* (Hutchinson, 1970); *The Macaroni Parson* (Hutchinson, 1973).

JOHNSON, DAVID: *Regency Revolution* (Compton Russell, 1974).

JONES, MICHAEL WYNN: *George Cruikshank, His Life and London* (Macmillan, 1978).

JUDGES, A. V.: *The Elizabethan Underworld* (Routledge and Kegan Paul, 1965).

LESLIE-MELVILLE, R.: *The Life and Work of Sir John Fielding* (Lincoln Williams, 1934).

MANDEVILLE, BERNARD: *An Enquiry into the Causes of the Frequent Executions at Tyburn (1725).* (The Augustan Reprint Society Publications No. 105, 1964).

MARKS, ALFRED: *Tyburn Tree: Its History and Annals* (Brown, Langham, 1905).

MAYHEW, H. and BINNEY, J.: *The Criminal Prisons of London* (Griffin, Bohn and Co., 1862).

NEWGATE CALENDAR (various editions).

O'DONNELL, BERNARD: *The Old Bailey and its Trials* (Theodore Brun, 1950).
Old Bailey Experience (anon.) (London, James Fraser, 1833).

PIERREPOINT, ALBERT: *Executioner Pierrepoint* (Harrap, 1974).

PUGH, R. B.: 'Newgate between two fires' (*Guildhall Studies in London History*, Vol. 3, Nos. 3 and 4, October 1978 and April 1979).

RADZINOWICZ, L.: *A History of English Criminal Law, Vols 1-4* (Stevens, 1948/1968).

RUMBELOW, D.: *I Spy Blue* (Macmillan, 1971).

SHARPE, R. R.: *Memorials of Newgate Gaol and the Sessions House, Old Bailey* (London, printed by Blades, 1907).

STROUD, DOROTHY: *George Dance, Architect, 1741-1825* (Faber and Faber, 1971).

TOLD, SILAS: *The Life of Mr Silas Told* (Epworth Press, 1954).

TUSSAUD, JOHN T: *The Romance of Madame Tussaud's* (Odhams Press, 1921).

TYBURN NUNS: *They died at Tyburn* (London, Tyburn Convent, 1961).

WAKEFIELD, E. GIBBON: *Facts relating to the punishment of death in the metropolis* (London, Wilson, 1832).

Index